Playing Roulette as a Business

PLAYING ROULETTE AS A BUSINESS

A PROFESSIONAL'S GUIDE TO BEATING THE WHEEL

R. J. SMART

A LYLE STUART BOOK
Published by Carol Publishing Group

A Lyle Stuart book
Published by Carol Publishing Group
Lyle Stuart is a registered trademark of Carol Communications, Inc.

Editorial, sales and distribution, rights and permissions inquiries should be addressed to Carol Publishing Group, 120 Enterprise Avenue, Secaucus, N.J. 07094

In Canada: Canadian Manda Group, One Atlantic Avenue, Suite 105, Toronto, Ontario M6K 3E7

Carol Publishing Group books may be purchased in bulk at special discounts for sales promotion, fund-raising, or educational purposes. Special editions can be created to specifications. For details, contact Special Sales Department, 120 Enterprise Avenue, Secaucus, N.J. 07094.

Manufactured in the United States of America
10 9 8 7 6 5 4 3 2 1

Library of Congress Cataloging-in-Publication Data

Smart, R. J.
Playing roulette as a business : a professional's guide to beating the wheel / R.J. Smart.
p. cm.
"A Lyle Stuart book."
ISBN 0-8184-0585-6 (pbk.)
1. Roulette. I. Title.
GV1309.S58 1996
795.2—dc20 96-25072
CIP

Contents

Introduction

I selected the pseudonym of R. J. Smart because I am, in truth, a Las Vegas casino dealer and I do not want my bosses—current or future—to know that one of their employees is responsible for the massive losses they will soon be incurring on the roulette table and I want you to be smart. As I write this book, I have no idea how many people will buy it and what the potential earnings from it may be. With that in mind, I still need my job and can't risk losing it by claiming credit for a system which I'm convinced will revolutionize the game of roulette and cause the casinos considerable consternation in the process.

Unlike many highfalutin' books on gaming that I've read which tend to be pedantic, I've hopefully written this in straightforward, easy-to-read English. I hope you enjoy reading this book as much as I've enjoyed writing it. And hey, go out and win some money. Who knows, one of these days you may end up at my roulette wheel. If you do, I won't be able to identify myself, but I'll get a big kick out of seeing you win money with this system.

Playing Roulette as a Business

1

The Game

As a dealer, I can assure you that roulette is undoubtedly the least played of all American casino table games. In fact, most people are reluctant to even learn the game. That is because a quick look at what appears to be a complicated layout turns them off. But roulette is, in fact, a very easy game to understand. It is also a very easy game at which to lose money.

There are not that many different bets on a roulette table. The roulette wheel is divided into thirty-eight equally sized segments, numbered 1 through 36 and 0 and 00. The roulette ball falls into one of the numbered segments on each spin, and players win or lose depending on whether they have placed any one of thirteen possible bets on that number.

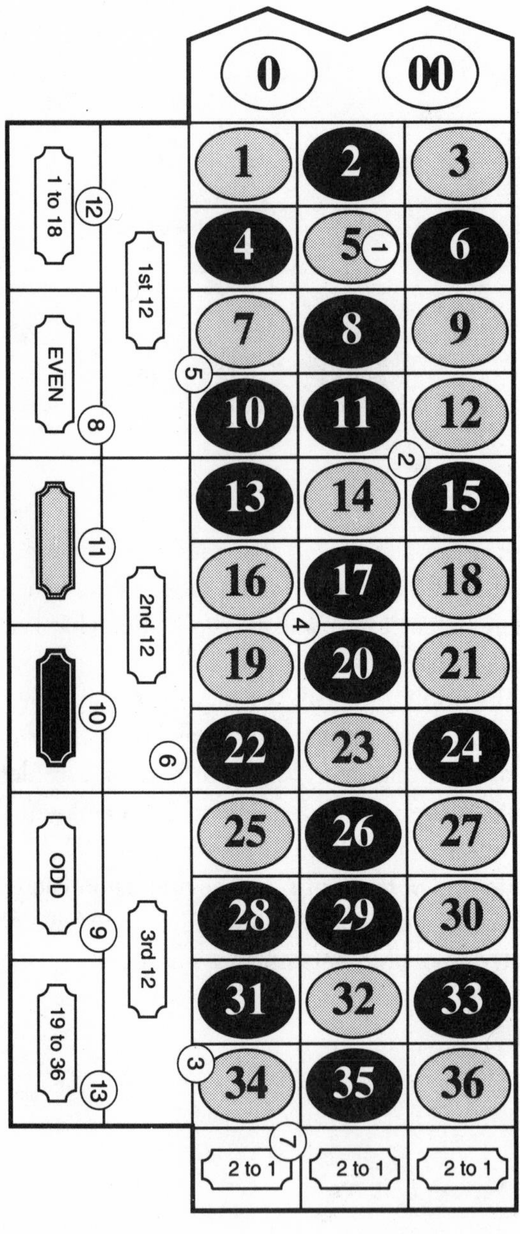
0
00
1
2
3
4
5
6
7
8
9
10
11
12
13
14
15
16
17
18
19
20
21
22
23
24
25
26
27
28
29
30
31
32
33
34
35
36
2 to 1
2 to 1
2 to 1
1 to 18
EVEN
ODD
19 to 36
1st 12
2nd 12
3rd 12

The thirteen bets and their payoffs are:

Bet	*Payoff Odds*
1. Straight-Up (money placed directly on a number):	35–1
2. Split (money placed on a line between two numbers):	17–1
3. Single-Row/Single-Street (money placed at the end of a row of three numbers):	11–1
3a. Special Three-Number (money placed at the tri-corner of the 0, 1, and 2; the 00, 2 and 3; or the 0, 00 and 2. Since these bets cover the same amount of numbers [three] as a Single-Row bet, the payoff is the same):	11–1
4. Four-Corner (money bet at the corner of four numbers):	8–1
5. Double-Row/Double-Street (money placed at the intersection of two rows which usually covers six different numbers):	5–1
5a. Special Double-Row/Double-Street (money placed at the intersection of the numbers 1 and 0 which covers only the five numbers 0, 00, 1, 2, and 3):	6–1

6. First 12, Second 12, or Third 12 (money placed in the long rectangular box adjoining either the first, second, or third group of 12 numbers, excluding the 0 and 00): 2–1
7. Column bets (money bet at the end of an individual column of numbers [excluding the 0 and 00]): 2–1

The above bets all cover specific sections of the roulette table; i.e., a specific number, a specific four numbers, or a specific column of numbers. The bets listed below cover 18 of the 36 numbers (excluding the 0 and 00) and pay even money (1–1):

8. Even (An even number hits, you win.)
9. Odd (An odd number hits, you win.)
10. Black (A black number hits, you win.)
11. Red (A red number hits, you win.)
12. 1–18 (One of the first half of the numbers hits, you win.)
13. 19–36 (One of the second half of the number hits, you win.)

There are a couple of important things that you should notice when looking at the above payoffs:

First, although there are thirty-eight potential winning Straight-Up bets (1 through 36, 0, and 00), a Straight-Up bet pays off at a rate of only 35 to 1, when the true odds should be 37 to 1. This lowered payoff is, of course, to the house's advantage.

The second important thing to notice is that the 1–1 bets do not cover the 0 or 00. This, too, is to the house's advantage.

(Again, do not worry about this house advantage. These particular bets are not even considered in our system.)

A house advantage exists for all roulette bets (it's how they can afford to build those fabulous palaces of pleasure). For example: True odds on a Four-Corner bet would be 17 to 2 based on the fact that, of the thirty-eight numbers, there are thirty-four potential losing numbers and only four potential winners (34 to 4 which, divided by 2, is 17 to 2). But the actual payoff is only 16 to 2 (or 8 to 1 if taken to the lowest denominator).

You can use the following mathematical computations to help you remember the odds for all the payoffs; but don't forget: the house *will* maintain an advantage! How do they do this? you ask yourself. The answer is, by using what I call the Rule of 36. The Rule of 36 simply means to eliminate the 0 and 00 from all computations and base odds determinations only on the thirty-six numbers that existed on a roulette wheel before the introduction of the 0 and 00. For example: If you bet a Double-Row computing the odds using only thirty-six numbers, you have thirty potential losing numbers and six potential winning numbers. They payoff of 30 to 6 broken down is 5 to 1.

This Rule of 36 applies even if you are betting on the 0 and 00, such as in the bet placed at the tri-corner of the 0, the 1, and the 2, as outlined above. In that particular bet, and using the Rule of 36 for determining odds purposes, you have thirty-three potential losing bets and three potential winning bets (33 to 3 breaks down to 11 to 1).

There you have it: all the roulette bets, what they cover, what the payoffs are, and how the odds for the payoffs are determined. Really quite simple, isn't it?

This being such a simple game, then, why is the roulette table so often avoided? One reason is because most people haven't read my insightful outline. But the main reason is that most people lose most of the time at roulette. Now let's find out how to not lose most of the time at roulette.

2

Beating the Game

As I implied before, a roulette dealer spends a lot of time standing around waiting for the occasional player to sit down. One day, while standing at my position at the table, I decided to look at the pattern of numbers on the wheel. That's when I noticed the phenomenon that is the basis of my system for beating the wheel. (See page 10 for illustration)

Notice that starting from the 2 and moving right, the numbers 0, 28, 9, 26, 30, 11, and 7 run consecutively. On the other side of the wheel, moving right consecutively from the 1, you find the 00, 27, 10, 25, 29, 12, and 8. How does this consecutive numbering pattern appear on the betting layout? See Fig. A, page 11.

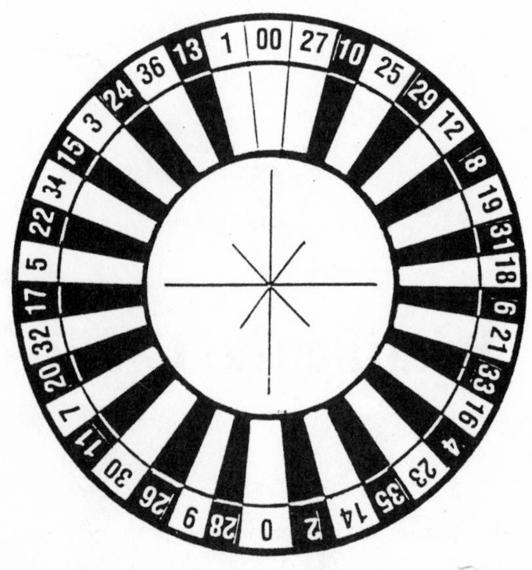

Remember the Double-Row bets from chapter 1? I'm sure you now see that you can make but three bets (see Fig. B on next page) and cover all the above sixteen numbers (with a bonus of the 3 added in)—a full 44.7 percent of the board. (Interestingly enough, and of great significance, these numbers hit at better than a 50 percent win rate! I believe the rate is higher because in a random pattern, you'd win 44.7 percent of the time, but our numbers run consecutively, thereby increasing the percentage of times they'll come up.)

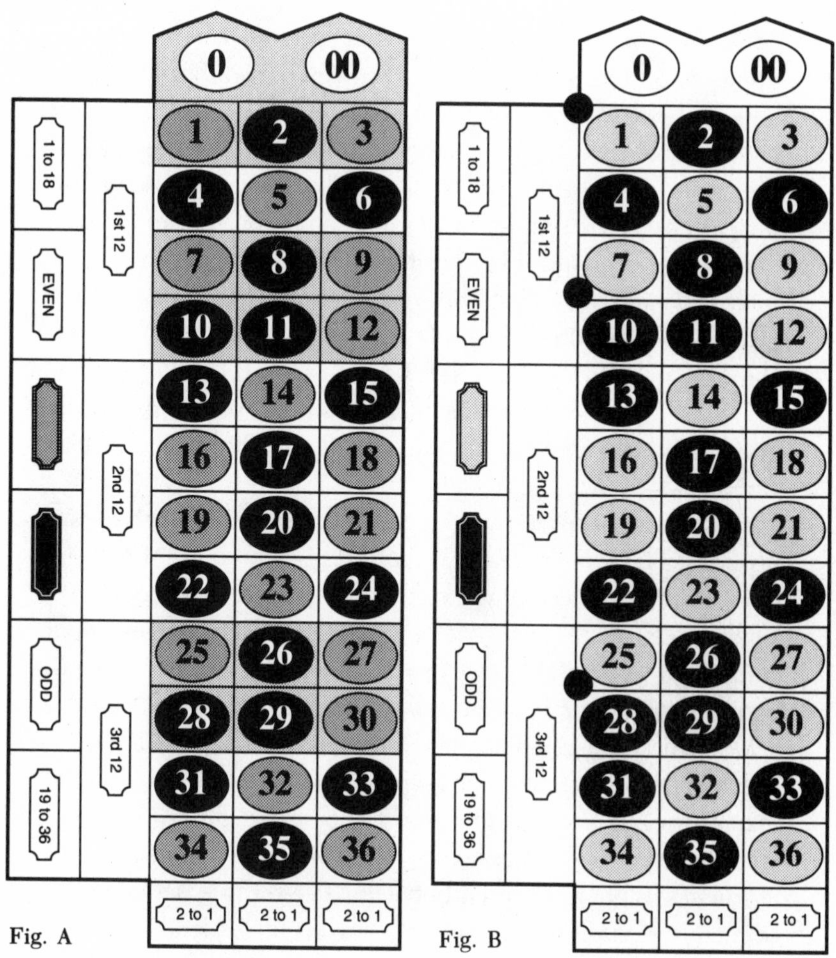
0
00
1 2 3
4 5 6
7 8 9
10 11 12
13 14 15
16 17 18
19 20 21
22 23 24
25 26 27
28 29 30
31 32 33
34 35 36
2 to 1
2 to 1
2 to 1
1 to 18
EVEN
ODD
19 to 36
1st 12
2nd 12
3rd 12

Fig. A

Fig. B

There you have it, three bets that cover 44.7 percent of the numbers on the roulette wheel. But, more significantly, three bets that cover almost one half of the wheel in two groups of eight consecutive numbers, each on directly opposite sides of the wheel! The game was undoubtedly designed this way on purpose by its creator, but it lay there undiscovered, to the best of my knowledge, until I noticed it. You can see that two of these bets—the one covering the 7 through the 12 and the one covering the 25 through the 30—pay at a 5-to-1 rate, and the third bet—covering the 0, 00, 1, 2, 3—pays 6 to 1.

Now, how do we use this information? If we make but three equal bets, we can cover all sixteen of those numbers (as well as the 3).

How much do we want to bet? Let's face it, although we are covering 44.7 percent of the wheel, this is gambling. At no time will our numbers come up exactly seventeen out of every thirty-eight spins as the 44.7 percent winning percentage would indicate. There will be stretches (relatively few and far between, I'm happy to report) when our numbers won't hit. How short? A look at the list of spin sequences beginning on page 16 shows that the longest stretch of nonwinners noted in the book is only six. (However, I must admit that I once lost eight in a row and got so angry that I threw away the spin sequence, so it's not listed in this book.) How far between? I've yet to experience two stretches of six losses in any one wagering session. With this knowledge in hand, we can now set about to develop a wagering system.

I've learned a thing or two as a dealer. One of them is, I do not care what casino game you are betting, the only chance you have to win consistently is by betting an upward progression. This is true for blackjack, craps, and roulette (I honestly do not know enough about baccarat to swear that this is true, but I strongly suspect so). This phenomenon is, in fact, the reason that casino table games have maximum bet limits. Logic dictates that if you keep doubling your bet, eventually you will hit a winner that earns you a profit. However, casinos know that if there is a maximum beyond which you cannot bet, eventually you will no longer be able to double your bet, and the losing streak that is surely coming will ultimately gobble you up. Let's look at a typical blackjack progression to illustrate what I mean.

Blackjack basically pays off at an even-money rate (granted there are chances to double down or split, and a blackjack itself pays 3 to 2, but you won't be hitting Double Downs, Splits, or Blackjacks if you're on a losing streak). For our purposes, let's say the table maximum is $500. With such a relatively high maximum, the table minimum would probably be $5. How many bets in a row would you need to lose to reach the table limit if you started with a $5 bet? Let's see:

Bet	*Outcome*	*Running Loss Total*
$5	Loss	$5
$10	Loss	$15
$20	Loss	$35
$40	Loss	$75
$80	Loss	$155
$160	Loss	$315
$320	Loss	$635

You've just hit the wall after your seventh bet! Because of the table limit, you cannot even make the eighth bet as listed above.

As a dealer, have I seen people lose seven bets in a row on a blackjack table? You'd better believe it! As a *player*, I've lost more than seven bets in a row. And to top all that bad news off, even if you win the fourth bet for $40, you still win only $5, because you've already lost $35 getting to the $40 bet.

But, happily, this bad-news progression doesn't apply to our roulette system. We win at better than a 1-to-1 rate because our payoffs come at either 5-to-1 or 6-to-1 odds! What, then, is a good example of progressive betting with our system? Here's one example, starting with a limited bankroll and playing conservatively (the figures below are expressed in dollars):

*Bet**	*Running Total***	*Win for the Spin****	*Profit*****
1.00/ 1.00/ 1.00	3.00	3.00/ 4.00	3.00/ 4.00
1.00/ 1.00/ 1.00	6.00	3.00/ 4.00	.00/ 1.00
2.00/ 2.00/ 2.00	12.00	6.00/ 8.00	.00/ 2.00
4.00/ 4.00/ 3.50	23.50	12.50/ 13.00	.50/ 1.00
8.00/ 8.00/ 7.00	46.50	25.00/ 26.00	1.50/ 2.50
16.00/16.00/14.00	92.50	50.00/ 52.00	3.50/ 5.50
32.00/32.00/28.00	184.50	100.00/104.00	7.50/11.50

*Bet: two Double-Row/Double-Street and Special Double-Row/ Double-Street bets *in order*.

**Running Total: the total amount bet up to that point.

***Win for the Spin: the amount you'd win on that particular spin. The first number is the win if a Double-Row hits; the second number is the win if the Special Double-Row hits.

****Profit: the *running total* (money already bet) subtracted from the *win per hand*. The first number is the profit if a Double-Row hits; the second is the profit if the Special Double-Row hits.

Since we do not have to double up our bets to make approximately the same amount of winnings as in blackjack, with our roulette system we can get seven bets for significantly less risk. But even the above betting progression requires a bankroll of $184.50. That's not just petty cash lying around. Is there another approach?

In a true progressive betting scheme, each *losing* bet is followed by a higher bet. After you hit a winner, you return to the initial bet of the progression. However, since this particular system is based on a preponderance of winning hits and most people begin with a limited bankroll, let's adjust our progression based on more than a 50 percent win rate.

What does a look at the spin sequences listed below show us? The number to the right is a running count of the total units won or lost. The left-hand numbers at the bottom of each column indicate the number of wins out of the total number of spins. The right-hand numbers indicate how many of the wins were 6 to 1 (the first number) and how many were 5 to 1 (the second number). (Throughout this book all winning spins are underlined.)

7
32
24
9
5
19
1
0
22
26
6
7
33
18
16
11
24
30
26
13
27
13
17
8
8
7
6
21
5
10
8
1
19
7
18
4

TOTAL 17/36
3/14

15
24
17
26
25
25
13
8
18
7
30
1
9
11
8
5
35
7
7
4
5
6
30
27
32
7
4
3
25
7
12
4
20
7
16
5
6
00
25

TOTAL 22/39
3/19

12
7
33
36
3
20
15
23
21
7
15
5
19
00
25
14
36
4
16
3
5
30
6
14
24
19
14
30
1
4

TOTAL 10/20
4/6

8
1
19
0
23
25
17
17
4
33
21
36
12
19
8
7
27
19
22
11
12
8
16
3
0
19

TOTAL 13/26
4/9

36
4
0
30
36
17
12
26
26
23
20
33
20
19
11
00
16
8
20
0
00
32
4
35
27
2
14
0
0
2
22
5

23
26
10
00
00
15
18
15
27
15
27
31
3
29

TOTAL 23/46
11/12

22
13
30
12
32
4
10
34
3
19
00
7
10
32
18
11
30
28
32
11
12
12
30
4
22
24
1
2
14
00
1
5

27
9
14
22
2
7
16

TOTAL 22/39
7/15

0
0
0
15
21
8
19
14
14
29
15
12
24
14
00
18
4
7
6
15
35
36
1
9
7
12
18
19
13
25
31
29

24
16
20
28
28
9
3
1
30
5

TOTAL 20/42
7/13

29
35
9
20
6
10
34
18
8
12
31
26
4
12
13
26
27
36
0
20
00
12
19
24
5
18
11
21
26
10
29
3

00
20
7
35
11
10
11
16
0
24
2
9
3
32
7
13
21
23
31
12
10
27

TOTAL 30/54
7/23

33

22

31

11

0

14

11

36

1

21

13

25

2

30

25

7

TOTAL 9/16

3/6

7

2

29

9

25

32

29

2

30

21

9

9

8

16

2

9

20

18

18

0

5

36

30

35

12

28

27

TOTAL 18/27

4/14

4
36
3
19
20
10
27
9
17
35
32
2
12
34
1
9

TOTAL 8/16
3/5

9
5
19
1
0
22
26
6
7
33
18
16
11
24
30
26
13
27
13
17
8
8
7
6
21
5
10
8

1
19
7
18
4

TOTAL 16/33
3/13

00	27	33		6
29	6	6		3
1	30	31		29
21	22	12		14
11	24	5		28
10	9	1		17
13	22	32		23
00	7	25		35
18	14	1		26
27	36	35		33
16	7	25		8
8	11	34		27
17	19	28		31
16	18	5		16
4	28	23		8
20	36	12		31
25	28	23		22
5	2	7		27
3	7	1		8
29	31	8		19
19	2	1		11
4	32	31		3
30	27	23		29
18	3	31		24
0	8	30		24
33	8	7		22
6	24	00		21
11	19	33		
33	21	3	TOTAL	59/123
24	35	3		17/42
4	7	21		
5	25	6		

10
13
13
35
3
24
18
4
36
2
25
13
26
18
31
12

TOTAL 6/16
2/4

9
12
35
31
12
6
28
1
0
3
00
33
16
32
8

TOTAL 9/15
4/5

16
4
28
27
22
18
10
21
2
25
3
11
14
3
7
2
26
27
27
21
00
5
20
15
27
30
12
30
29
32
11

TOTAL 20/31
5/15

10
16
1
20
11
5
23
24
27
9
33
17
13
18
9

TOTAL 6/15
1/5

2
9
24
2
33
9
3
28
16
10
5
19
36
35
25
23
20
3
0
0
0
6
14
1
4
30
20
7
28
27
00
3

3
15
11
0
8
3
10
32
14
15
24
15
10

TOTAL 26/45
13/13

30
31
10
27
19
17
10
0
2
17
35
16
12
25
1
15
0
16
0
5
31
0
15
12
00
00
21
3
1
4
36
17

9
15
28
30
5
34

TOTAL 20/38
10/10

<u>8</u>		35
34		24
<u>26</u>		<u>30</u>
33		6
17		<u>8</u>
<u>2</u>		32
31		17
18		<u>3</u>
<u>12</u>		33
<u>30</u>		<u>00</u>
<u>8</u>		16
17		<u>9</u>
<u>12</u>		<u>10</u>
5		34
34		18
19		31
4		35
<u>3</u>		<u>7</u>
<u>12</u>		<u>28</u>
32		
<u>7</u>	TOTAL	22/51
<u>8</u>		4/18
<u>26</u>		
31		
32		
15		
<u>10</u>		
31		
6		
4		
<u>7</u>		
23		

The first thing to make a note of is this: Out of 739 spins, 376 are winners and only 363 are losers. This would seem to be approximately a 50.8 percent win rate. But remember one important fact: Of those 376 winners, 115 are 6-to-1 Special Double-Row hits. The 115 6-to-1-odds wins actually add to the percentage of victories, because 115 times you get an added 33 percent profit. Thirty-three percent of 115 equals 38, so, in reality, the 376 wins pay like 414 wins. Having 414 wins in 736 spins equals a 55 percent win rate.

The other important thing to note is that there are 96 winning streaks of varying lengths, 96 one-spin losing streaks, 43 two-spin losing streaks, 31 three-spin losing streaks, 13 four-spin losing streaks, 3 five-spin losing streaks, and 1 six-spin losing streak (only 91 losing streaks of more than one loss in a row).

Based on the above information and hours of studying various betting systems to determine the best, *most economical* way to earn a profit at minimal risk, the betting progression I prefer—one that minimizes risk while maintaining an acceptable profit rate—is a 1-1-1-2-4-6-8-16-32 (153 units) progression where 1 indicates that one unit should be bet on each of the three Double-Row bets. If our unit is $1.00, with $1.00 bet on each of the three Double-Row bets (total of $3.00 bet), if 7 through 12 or 25 through 30 hits, it pays $3.00 based on the fact that the win pays $5.00 (at 5 to 1) but you lose the $2.00 you bet on the two Double-Rows that didn't hit. If the 0, 00, 1, 2, or 3 hits (which occurs approximately 30 percent of the time), you win $4.00 based on the fact that you get $6.00 for the win but lose $2.00 on the two other Double-Row bets that didn't hit.

What are the particular advantages of this betting progression? The progression is based on eliminating a percentage of the losses incurred during a losing streak by increasing the bet when it is advantageous, but not on eliminating all the losses in any particular cold stretch. If we try to eliminate all the losses, the betting progression accelerates too quickly for a modest bankroll. And, of greater significance, it is not necessary to eliminate all losses, because we will recover any money lost in a cold stretch during winning streaks which occur more often than extended losing stretches.

Earlier we looked at the big picture when it comes to the profit added when the Special Double-Row hits (38 added wins based on 115 Special Double-Row wins). Now, let's look more closely at the numbers. On average 30 percent (5 out of every 17) of our wins will be Special Double-Row (0-00-1-2-3) wins. We already know that those Special Double-Row wins add a profit of 33 percent. In general, then, a $3.00 win following a $3.00 loss seems to eliminate both one win and one loss from the spin sequence. Since this happens 96 times, it would seem that 376 wins play like 280 wins, and 363 losses play like 267 losses. But, because 30 percent of the wins after the 96 one spin losing streaks pay at a 6-to-1 rate (a 33.3 percent increase in profit—$4.00 instead of $3.00), this loss-followed-by-a-win ratio actually increases the working number of wins by 10 (96 wins × 30 percent [the average number of times the 0-00-1-2-3 will hit] × 33.3 percent [the increased profit if the 0-00-1-2-3 hit]). So, in truth, the 376 wins pay like 290 wins, but the 363 losses still pay like 225 losses. This works out to a 52 percent win percentage.

The same applies to three $1.00 Double-Row bets after two losses. Forty-three times after two losses (according to our spin sequences), you'll win. How does this play out when comparing wins to losses? We start with our base of 376 wins and 363 losses; eliminating both 43 wins and 43 losses from that total yields 333 wins and 320 losses. But remember, because 30 percent of the wins show a 33.3 percent profit, we must increase our win total by 4 units (43 × 30 percent × 33.3 percent), assuming 1 unit is bet on each Double-Row—increasing our win total to 337 units. So, when we win after two losses, the win percentage is 51.3 percent (337 wins as opposed to 320 losses). This is slightly lower than the average percentage gain but acceptable if we want to minimize the bankroll we start with.

Continuing on, after three losses in a row, we increase the bet to 2 units per Double-Row. Based upon the spin sequences in this book, an increase to 2 units after the third loss in a row will win 31 times. But, because these 31 wins are at double the rate of the previous two bets, they essentially eliminate twice as many losses—62. Additionally, the 33.3 percent increase 30 percent of the time on 31 wins adds 3 wins. This progression eliminates 62 losses but only eliminates 28 wins (31 wins lost minus 3 additional wins) which plays as 388 wins as opposed to 301 losses—a 53.6 percent win percentage.

I won't bore you anymore with the mathematics involved with the rest of the 1-1-1-2-4-6-8-16-32 progression; however, each bet is made to eliminate enough losses to maintain an acceptable win percentage.

Okay, there you have it—a betting progression designed to increase profits while minimizing bankroll risks. How does it play out using the spin sequences in this book—each of which actually occurred at a Las Vegas casino? Let's see on the next page. The first number in each column is the number that hit, the second number is the running win total, and the third number is the number of units bet.

3

The 1-1-1-2-4-6-8-16-32 Betting Progression at Work

Listed below is one spin sequence listed in three columns so it will fit on one page. The second number in each column is the running win/lose total expressed in dollars. (This spin sequence will be the example for variations of the betting system discussed throughout this book.)

00	4	1 unit bet*	36	−1	1 unit bet*	1	23	1 unit bet*
29	7	1 unit bet	7	2	1 unit bet	8	26	1 unit bet
1	11	1 unit bet	11	5	1 unit bet	1	30	1 unit bet
21	8	1 unit bet	19	2	1 unit bet	31	27	1 unit bet
11	11	1 unit bet	18	−1	1 unit bet	23	24	1 unit bet
10	14	1 unit bet	28	2	1 unit bet	31	21	1 unit bet
13	11	1 unit bet	16	−1	1 unit bet	30	27	2 units bet
00	15	1 unit bet	28	2	1 unit bet	7	30	1 unit bet
18	12	1 unit bet	2	6	1 unit bet	00	34	1 unit bet

27	15	1 unit bet	7	9	1 unit bet	33	31	1 unit bet
16	12	1 unit bet	31	6	1 unit bet	3	35	1 unit bet
8	15	1 unit bet	2	10	1 unit bet	3	39	1 unit bet
17	12	1 unit bet	32	7	1 unit bet	21	36	1 unit bet
16	9	1 unit bet	27	10	1 unit bet	6	33	1 unit bet
4	6	1 unit bet	3	14	2 units bet	6	30	1 unit bet
20	0	2 units bet	8	17	4 units bet	3	38	2 units bet
25	12	4 units bet	8	20	1 unit bet	29	41	1 unit bet
5	9	1 unit bet	24	17	1 unit bet	14	38	1 unit bet
3	13	1 unit bet	19	14	1 unit bet	28	41	1 unit bet
29	16	1 unit bet	21	11	1 unit bet	17	38	1 unit bet
19	13	1 unit bet	35	5	2 units bet	23	35	1 unit bet
4	10	1 unit bet	7	17	4 units bet	35	32	1 unit bet
30	13	1 unit bet	25	20	1 unit bet	26	38	2 units bet
18	10	1 unit bet	33	17	1 unit bet	33	35	1 unit bet
0	14	1 unit bet	6	14	1 unit bet	8	38	1 unit bet
33	11	1 unit bet	31	11	1 unit bet	27	41	1 unit bet
6	8	1 unit bet	12	17	2 units bet	31	38	1 unit bet
11	11	1 unit bet	5	14	1 unit bet	16	35	1 unit bet
33	8	1 unit bet	1	18	1 unit bet	8	38	1 unit bet
24	5	1 unit bet	32	15	1 unit bet	31	35	1 unit bet
4	2	1 unit bet	25	18	1 unit bet	22	32	1 unit bet
5	−4	2 units bet	1	22	1 unit bet	27	35	1 unit bet
27	8	4 units bet	35	19	1 unit bet	8	38	1 unit bet
6	5	1 unit bet	25	22	1 unit bet	19	35	1 unit bet
30	8	1 unit bet	34	19	1 unit bet	11	38	1 unit bet
22	5	1 unit bet	28	22	1 unit bet	3	42	1 unit bet
24	2	1 unit bet	5	19	1 unit bet	29	45	1 unit bet
9	5	1 unit bet	23	16	1 unit bet	24	42	1 unit bet
22	2	1 unit bet	12	19	1 unit bet	24	39	1 unit bet
7	5	1 unit bet	23	16	1 unit bet	22	36	1 unit bet
14	2	1 unit bet	7	19	1 unit bet	21	30	2 units bet
						59/123		

*On each Double-Row

Notice one significant fact: In this particular sitting, even though there were actually more losses (64) than wins (59), I still won 30 units because of the betting progression and the fact that almost 30 percent of the time (17 out of 59 wins) I earned an extra 33 percent!

If the unit we are betting is $1.00, we've made a $30.00 profit in about two hours. (At the time of this particular gaming session, I was the only player at the table, which accounts for getting over 120 rolls in two hours.) But if the unit was $6.00, we would have won $180.00 in two hours.

Let's look at more spin sequences—all actually played at a Las Vegas casino. All spin sequences are using the 1-1-1-2-4-6-8-16-32 betting progression:

<u>7</u>	3
32	0
24	−3
<u>9</u>	0
5	−3
19	−6
<u>1</u>	−2
<u>0</u>	2
22	−1
<u>26</u>	2
6	−1
<u>7</u>	2
33	−1
18	−4
16	−7
<u>11</u>	−1
24	−4
<u>30</u>	−1
<u>26</u>	2
13	−1
<u>27</u>	2
13	−1
17	−4
<u>8</u>	−1
<u>8</u>	2
<u>7</u>	5
6	2
21	−1
5	−4
<u>10</u>	2
<u>8</u>	5
<u>1</u>	9

	19	6
	<u>7</u>	9
	18	6
	4	3
TOTAL	17/36	
	3/14	

15	−3
24	−6
17	−9
<u>26</u>	−3
<u>25</u>	0
<u>25</u>	3
13	0
<u>8</u>	3
18	0
<u>7</u>	3
<u>30</u>	6
<u>1</u>	10
<u>9</u>	13
<u>11</u>	16
<u>8</u>	19
5	16
35	13
<u>7</u>	16
<u>7</u>	19
4	16
5	13
6	10
<u>30</u>	16
<u>27</u>	19
32	16
<u>7</u>	19
4	16
<u>3</u>	20
<u>25</u>	23
<u>7</u>	26
<u>12</u>	29
4	26

	20	23
	<u>7</u>	26
	16	23
	5	20
	6	17
	<u>00</u>	25
	<u>25</u>	28
TOTAL	22/39	
	3/19	

0	4
0	8
0	12
15	9
21	6
8	9
19	6
14	3
14	0
29	6
15	3
12	6
24	3
14	0
00	4
18	1
4	−2
7	1
6	−2
15	−5
35	−8
36	−14
1	2
9	5
7	8
12	11
18	8
19	5
13	2
25	8
31	5
29	8
24	5
16	2
20	−1
28	5
28	8
9	11
3	15
1	19
30	22
5	19

TOTAL 20/42
7/13

36	−3
4	−6
0	−2
30	1
36	−2
17	−5
12	−2
26	1
26	4
23	1
20	−2
33	−5
20	−11
19	−23
11	− 5
00	− 1
16	− 4
8	− 1
20	− 4
0	0
00	4
32	1
4	−2
35	−5
27	1
2	5
14	2
0	6
0	10
2	14
22	11
5	8
23	5
26	11
10	14
00	18
00	22
15	19
18	16
15	13
27	19
15	16
27	19
31	16
3	20
29	23

TOTAL 23/46
11/12

22	−3
13	−6
30	−3
12	0
32	−3
4	−6
10	−3
34	−6
3	−2
19	−5
00	−1
7	2
10	5
32	2
18	−1
11	2
30	5
28	8
32	5
11	8
12	11
12	14
30	17
4	14
22	11
24	8
1	16
2	20
14	17
00	21
1	25
5	22

	27	25
	9	28
	14	25
	22	22
	2	26
	7	29
	16	26
TOTAL	22/39	
	7/15	

	12	3
	7	6
	33	3
	36	0
	3	4
	20	1
	15	−2
	23	−5
	21	−11
	7	1
	15	−2
	5	−5
	19	−8
	00	0
	25	3
	14	0
	36	−3
	4	−6
	16	−12
	3	4
	5	1
	30	4
	6	1
	14	−2
	24	−5
	19	−11
	14	−23
	30	−5
	1	−1
	4	−4
TOTAL	10/30	
	4/6	

33	−3
22	−6
31	−9
11	−3
0	1
14	−2
11	1
36	−2
1	2
21	−1
13	−4
25	−1
2	3
30	6
25	9
7	12

TOTAL 9/16
3/6

7	3
2	7
29	10
9	13
25	16
32	13
29	16
2	20
30	23
21	20
9	23
9	26
8	29
16	26
2	30
9	33
20	30
18	27
18	24
0	32
5	29
36	26
30	29
35	26
12	29
28	32
27	35

TOTAL 18/27
4/14

4	−3
36	−6
3	−2
19	−5
20	−8
10	−5
27	−2
9	1
17	−2
35	−5
32	−8
2	0
12	3
34	0
1	4
9	7
TOTAL	8/16
	3/5

2	3
9	6
24	3
2	7
33	4
9	7
3	11
28	14
16	11
10	14
5	11
19	8
36	5
35	−1
25	11
23	8
20	5
3	9
0	13
0	17
0	21
6	18
14	15
1	19
4	16
30	19
20	16
7	19
28	22
27	25
00	29
3	33

	3	37
	15	34
	11	37
	0	41
	8	44
	3	48
	10	51
	32	48
	14	45
	15	42
	24	36
	15	24
	10	42
TOTAL	26/45	
	13/13	

30	3
31	0
10	3
27	6
19	3
17	0
10	3
0	7
2	11
17	8
35	5
16	2
12	8
25	11
1	15
15	12
0	16
16	13
0	17
5	14
31	11
0	15
15	12
12	15
00	19
00	23
21	20
3	24
1	28
4	25
36	22
17	19
9	25
15	22
28	25
30	28
5	25
34	22

TOTAL 20/38
10/10

8	3
34	0
26	3
33	0
17	−3
2	1
31	−2
18	−5
12	−2
30	1
8	4
17	1
12	4
5	1
34	−2
19	−5
4	−11
3	5
12	8
32	5
7	8
8	11
26	14
31	11
32	8
15	5
10	11
31	8
6	5
4	2
7	8
23	5
35	2
24	−1
30	5
6	2
8	5
32	2
17	−1
3	3
33	0
00	4
16	1
9	4
10	7
34	4
18	1
31	−2
35	−8
7	4
28	7

TOTAL 22/51
4/18

9	3
12	6
35	3
31	0
12	3
6	0
28	3
1	7
0	11
3	15
00	19
33	16
16	13
32	10
8	16

TOTAL 9/15
4/5

16	−3
4	−6
28	−3
27	0
22	−3
18	−6
10	−3
21	−6
2	−2
25	1
3	5
11	8
14	5
3	9
7	12
2	16
26	19
27	22
27	25
21	22
00	26
5	23
20	20
15	17
27	23
30	26
12	29
30	32
29	35
32	32
11	35

TOTAL 20/31
5/15

10	3
16	0
1	4
20	1
11	4
5	1
23	−2
24	−5
27	1
9	4
33	1
17	−2
13	−5
18	−11
9	1
14	

TOTAL 6/16
1/5

8	3
1	7
19	4
0	8
23	5
25	8
17	5
17	2
4	−1
33	−7
21	−19
36	−37
12	−15
19	−18
8	−15
7	−12
27	−9
19	−12
22	−15
11	−12
12	−9
8	−6
16	−9
3	−5
0	−1
19	−4

TOTAL 13/26
4/9

29	3
35	0
9	3
20	0
6	−3
10	0
34	−3
18	−6
8	−3
12	0
31	−3
26	0
4	−3
12	0
13	−3
26	0
27	3
36	0
0	4
20	1
00	5
12	8
19	5
24	2
5	−1
18	−7
11	5
21	2
26	5
10	8
29	11
3	15

00	19
20	16
7	19
35	16
11	19
10	22
11	25
16	22
0	26
24	23
2	27
9	30
3	34
32	31
7	34
13	31
21	28
23	25
31	19
12	31
10	34
27	37

TOTAL 30/54
7/23

9	3
5	0
19	−3
1	1
0	5
22	2
26	5
6	2
7	5
33	2
18	−1
16	−4
11	2
24	−1
30	2
26	5
13	2
27	5
13	2
17	−1
8	2
8	5
7	8
6	5
21	2
5	−1
10	5
8	8
1	12
19	9
7	12
18	9
4	6

TOTAL 16/33
3/13

10	3		25	6
13	0		13	3
13	−3		26	6
35	−6		18	3
3	2		31	0
24	−1		12	3
18	−4			
4	−7	TOTAL	6/16	
36	−13		2/4	
2	3			

As you can see, in twenty sessions of varying lengths, there were only two losing sessions, totaling only 8 units. On the other hand, there were eighteen winning sessions, which earned a total of 352 units for a total profit of 344 units; $344.00 dollars if our unit is $1.00. But let's say our unit is $5.00; if it were, we'd win $1,720.00!

But the real power of this system is the minimal losses we suffer even when we have a bad run. Look at the second spin sequence. In that particular sitting, I won only one third of my bets but suffered a loss of only 4 units by eliminating losses using the bet progression. Not bad. Now look at the last spin sequence, the only other losing session. I won as many as I lost, but in the middle of that spin sequence, I suffered the only six-loss-in-a-row stretch and yet still lost only 4 units. Again, an acceptable loss considering the numerous winning sessions that surrounded it.

But, don't ever forget, this is gambling. To date, I've only experienced a losing streak of more than six one time (not listed, as mentioned before). But even then, I have eighteen winning sessions and only three losing sessions.

4

Getting Started

Perhaps I should take some time to explain how the novice roulette player gets started. You now know where to place your bets, in what amounts, and why you are doing so. But how do you get started?

When you approach the roulette table, you will see stacks of checks (gaming terminology for chips) behind the wheel, separated into different groups by color. Each stack is always twenty checks high, and there are normally fifteen stacks of each color. Unlike blackjack or craps checks, which have their value printed on them, roulette checks show no value. The player determines the value of roulette checks. In smaller casinos, you can usually purchase and play with checks worth $.25 each, and those casinos generally require you to purchase a minimum of $5.00 worth of checks. If you buy $5.00 worth of $.25 checks, the dealer will hand you one stack of checks. In addition to the requirement to buy in for $5.00, most smaller casinos require you to bet a minimum of $1.00 spread around the "inside" (for example, one check on 7, two on 15, one on the

35/36 Split) or $1.00 (four checks) on any individual "outside" bet. (The "inside" is that area with the numbers 1 through 36, 0, and 00 on it. The "outside" is the remainder of the layout—the row with the Black and Red bets on it; the row with the first, second, and third 12 bets; and the 2-to-1 column bets.)

If you want $10.00 worth of $.25 checks, the dealer will give you two stacks of twenty checks. And, just as logically, if you want $5.00 worth of $.50 checks, the dealer will give you only one half of one stack of checks—and do something else. After you've bought in for a value higher than the table minimum, the dealer will take one check of your color and a "lammer" (a round button with a number on it)—in this case a 10—and place the check with the lammer on top of it on the wall of the roulette wheel. This shows the floorperson—the dealer's boss—that each of your stacks is worth $10.00. (The dealer won't mark buy-ins for $.25 checks because most players play the table minimum, and the roulette wheel wall would get overloaded. If only your check is marked, the floorperson will know that all the other players are playing $.25 checks and see that you are playing $.50 checks.)

Mid-sized casinos require buying in for a minimum of $10.00 worth of $.50 checks (you can't even buy $.25 checks). If you buy in for the minimum, you will receive one stack—twenty checks. Since you are playing for the table minimum, the dealer will not mark it with a lammer. If you want each check to be worth $1.00, the dealer will mark one of your checks with a 20 lammer and place it on the wall of the wheel. This informs the floorperson that each of your checks is worth $1.00 (the 20 lammer indicates that each of your stacks is worth $20.00).

By the way, lammers are also used to keep a running count of the total cash paid for checks, per shift, at the roulette wheel;

they're usually set in a shot glass on the table. If you buy in for $50.00, the dealer will put a 50 lammer into the shot glass so the floorperson can quickly count the total amount of cash spent for checks if he needs that information for accounting purposes.

Another important thing to know is that once the ball falls into a number, the dealer will mark it with a marker, sweep off the losing bets, then pay the winning bets. For our system's bets (all on the inside), the dealer will pay you directly, although the dealer pays the outside bets where they lay. You will see that the other players don't collect their outside bets' winnings until after the dealer removes the marker from the layout and says, "Place your bets." You, too, should wait until the dealer removes the marker and says, "Place your bets," before you make your next bets.

5

Variations on the Same Theme

3-3-1 VARIATION

I hope you noticed that three of the numbers in our system are either on the periphery of the grouping or, in the case of the 3, not even in the grouping. If you want to increase your profit per hit but at the same time reduce the number of wins, try these three bets: 3 units on the 7–12, 3 units on the 25–30, and 1 unit on the 0–00 Split. These three bets cover 36.8 percent of the numbers on the roulette wheel. But more significantly, they are three bets that cover more than one-third of the wheel in two groups of seven consecutive numbers, each on directly opposite sides of the wheel!

The 7–12 and 25–30 Double-Row bets pay at 5 to 1. And a 0–00 Split bet pays 17 to 1. Doesn't really seem to be much correlation, does there? But, interestingly enough, there is a direct ratio between these two bets that I discovered only over the course of some time.

And what is this relationship between two 5-to-1 bets and one 17-to-1 bet? If you bet them at exactly the 3-to-3-to-1 ratio I described above, with the higher bets on the Double-Rows and the lower bet on the 0-00 Split bet, the payoff is the same. For example, bet $3.00 on the two Double-Row bets and $1.00 on the 0-00 Split bet. Let's say the 7 hits. You would win $15.00 on the Double-Row bet placed between the 7 and the 10, but lose $3.00 on the Double-Row bet between the 25 and 28 and lose $1.00 on the 0-00 Split bet. Fifteen dollars minus $4.00 is an $11.00 profit. Let's do the same bet with a different winner, the 0. You'd win $17.00 on the 0-00 Split bet, but lose $3.00 each on the Double Row 7–10 and the Double-Row 25–28. Seventeen dollars minus $6.00 is also an $11.00 winner!

This mathematical truism applies to all 3-to-3-to-1 ratio bets placed as described. For example, a $10.50-$10.50-$3.50 bet pays $38.50 (the $52.50 you're paid on the winning Double-Row bet minus $14.00 [the $10.50 Double-Row bet you didn't hit plus the $3.50 0-00 Split bet you missed]) if the 7–12 or 25–30 hits, and $38.50 if the 0-00 Split hits ($59.50—the $3.50 bet times 17—minus the $21.00 you would lose on the two Double Row bets). Interesting isn't it?

Well, you now have the numbers you want to bet and the ratio at which you want to bet them for this particular variation. What's next?

How much we want to bet, of course. Let's face it, although we are covering 36.8 percent of the wheel, this is gambling. At no time will our numbers come up exactly one out of every three spins as the 36.8 percent winning percentage would indicate. There will be stretches when our numbers won't hit. How short? The longest stretch of nonwinners I've experienced is nine—and that only once. How far between? I've yet to experience two such stretches in any one wagering session (please look at the spin sequence listed below). With this knowledge in hand, we can now set about to develop a wagering system.

What then is a good betting progression for this variation? Here's one example starting with a limited bankroll. (Notice that the first bet is not at a 3-to-3-to-1 ratio. This is because a smaller initial bet will save you money at the higher levels.) The initial betting progression listed below starts at $1.00/$1.00/$.50 as if you are playing on a $2.00 minimum table using the minimum $.50 chip value (all figures below are expressed in dollars):

*Bet**	*Running Total***	*Win for the Spin****	*Profit*****
1.00/ 1.00/ .50	2.50	3.50/ 6.50	3.50/6.50
1.50/ 1.50/ .50	6.00	5.50/ 5.50	3.00/3.00
3.00/ 3.00/1.00	13.00	11.00/11.00	5.00/5.00
4.50/ 4.50/1.50	23.50	16.50/16.50	3.50/3.50
7.50/ 7.50/2.50	41.00	27.50/27.50	4.00/4.00
12.00/12.00/3.00	68.00	45.00/45.00	4.00/4.00
21.00/21.00/7.00	117.00	77.00/77.00	9.00/9.00

*Bet: the two Double-Row bets and the 0-00 Split, *in order*.

**Running Total: the total amount bet up to that point.

***Win for the Spin: the amount you'd win on that particular spin. The first number is the win if a Double-Row hits; the second number is the win if the 0-00 Split hits.

****Profit: the *running total* from the row above (money already bet) subtracted from the *win for the Spin*. The first number is the profit if a Double-Row hits; the second is the profit if the 0-00 Split hits.

All right then, as I stated before, this is gambling. You will have more than seven losses in a row at some time in your wagering. What do I recommend when this happens? There are two possible approaches. With a limited bankroll, my advice is to simply have a cutoff point of losses after which you no longer increase your bet. Take the loss, wait until the losing streak ends (until one of our system numbers hits), then start again with the same bets. Since losing streaks are few and far between, perhaps the best advice I can give you is to find a casino that uses a roulette number board (a board that lists the last sixteen numbers rolled), wait until a losing streak comes *and* ends before you start your round of wagering, then start betting. (Bear one very important fact in mind: Roulette number boards are not infallible. I have seen them register the wrong number on more than one occasion, with no correction attempted.)

For those with a healthier bankroll, the second possibility is to double up after a losing streak. Using the above listed betting scheme as an example, after a losing streak, you could start with a $2.00/$2.00/$1.00 wager and proceed upward from there:

Bet	*Running Total*	*Win for the Spin*	*Profit*
2.00/ 2.00/ 1.00	5.00	7.00/ 13.00	7.00/13.00
3.00/ 3.00/ 1.50	12.50	11.00/ 11.00	6.00/ 6.00
6.00/ 6.00/ 2.00	26.50	22.00/ 22.00	9.50/ 9.50
9.00/ 9.00/ 3.00	37.50	32.00/ 32.00	5.50/ 5.50
12.00/12.00/ 4.00	65.50	44.00/ 44.00	6.50/ 6.50
21.00/21.00/ 7.00	114.50	77.00/ 77.00	11.50/11.50
33.00/33.00/11.00	191.50	121.00/121.00	6.50/ 6.50

I didn't bet the first eight because I usually wait for one of our numbers to hit before I start. Before the next spin, I bet $1.00 on each of the two Double-Rows and $.50 on the 0-00 Split. I lost this $2.50 when the 34 hit. Then I bet $1.50 on each of the two Double-Rows and $.50 on the 0-00 Split. I won this bet when the 26 hit, so the dealer gave me $5.50, but I'd already lost $2.50 the spin before. My profit for those two spins is $5.50 minus $2.50, which is $3.00 as indicated in the Profit column and by the +3.00 next to the 26. Then I lost five progressive bets in a row when the 33, 17, 2, 31, and 18 hit for a running total loss of $41.00. Then I hit a 12 with $12.00 on each Double-Row and 4.00 on 0-00. My win per (that) hand was $45.00, but, since I'd already lost 41.00 getting to that sixth bet, my profit was $4.00. Since I'd won $3.00 earlier when the 26 hit, after the 12 hit my total profit was $7.00 as indicated by the +7.00 next to the 12.

Let's see how both betting systems would work—just continuing the original betting progression or doubling up. The following spin sequence is one that actually happened with the winnings listed alongside. I've included the betting progression chart with the following spin sequences so you won't have to change pages every few seconds. (Every spin sequence really occurred unless otherwise noted.)

8 I wait for one of our numbers to hit before I start wagering.
34
26 +3.00 (second bet listed below, which wins a profit of $3.00)
33
17
2
31
18
12 +7.00
30 +10.50
8 +14.00
17
12 +17.00
5
34
19
4
3

Bet	*Running Total*	*Win for the Spin*	*Profit*
1.00/ 1.00/ .50	2.50	3.50/ 6.50	3.50/6.50
1.50/ 1.50/ .50	6.00	5.50/ 5.50	3.00/3.00
3.00/ 3.00/1.00	13.00	11.00/11.00	5.00/5.00
4.50/ 4.50/1.50	23.50	16.50/16.50	3.50/3.50
7.50/ 7.50/2.50	41.00	27.50/27.50	4.00/4.00
12.00/12.00/3.00	68.00	45.00/45.00	4.00/4.00
21.00/21.00/7.00	117.00	77.00/77.00	9.00/9.00

12	+21.00	(a close one, but percentages worked out)
32		
7	+24.00	
8	+27.50	
26	+31.00	
31		
32		
15		
10	+34.50	
31		
6		
4		
7	+38.00	
23		
35		
24		
30	+41.50	
6		
8	+44.50	
32		
17		
3		
33		
00	+48.50	
16		
9	+51.50	
10	+55.00	
34		
18		
31		
35		
7	+59.00	
28	+62.50	

Let's add a six-in-a-row losing streak which *didn't occur* and stop betting after the sixth loss in a row.

8	I wait for one of our numbers to hit before I start wagering.	
34		
26	+3.00	(second bet listed below, which wins a profit of $3.00)
33		

Bet	Running Total	Win for the Spin	Profit
1.00/ 1.00/ .50	2.50	3.50/ 6.50	3.50/6.50
1.50/ 1.50/ .50	6.00	5.50/ 5.50	3.00/3.00
3.00/ 3.00/1.00	13.00	11.00/11.00	5.00/5.00
4.50/ 4.50/1.50	23.50	16.50/16.50	3.50/3.50
7.50/ 7.50/2.50	41.00	27.50/27.50	4.00/4.00
12.00/12.00/3.00	68.00	45.00/45.00	4.00/4.00
21.00/21.00/7.00	117.00	77.00/77.00	9.00/9.00

17
2
31
18
12 +7.00
30 +10.50
8 +14.00
17
12 +17.00
5
34
19
4
3
[13] −51.00 Artificially added!! ($68.00 loss minus $17.00 ahead)
12 ⟵ You didn't bet this. It's the number to restart betting after.
32
7 −47.50
8 −44.00
26 −40.50
31
32
15
10 −37.00
31
6
4
7 −33.50
23
35
24
30 −30.50
6
8 −26.50
32
17
3
33
00 −23.50
16
9 −20.00
10 −16.00
34
18

31
35
7 −12.50
28 −9.00*

*Although the last figure is still in the negative, remember this was a setup that never really occurred. I hope you see that you can quickly recover even after what I call a *catastrophic failure*—my contribution to highfalutin terminology.

Let's stay with the added six-in-a-row losing streak but double up after the *catastrophic failure.*

		Bet	Running Total	Win for the Spin	Profit
8		Again, wait for one of our numbers before starting to wager.			
34					
26	+3.00	(second bet listed below, which wins for a profit of $3.00)			
33					
17					
2					
31					
18		2.00/ 2.00/ 1.00	5.00		7.00/13.00
12	+7.00	3.00/ 3.00/ 1.50	12.50	11.00/ 11.00	6.00/ 6.00
30	+10.50	6.00/ 6.00/ 2.00	26.50	22.00/ 22.00	9.50/ 9.50
8	+14.00	9.00/ 9.00/ 3.00	37.50	32.00/ 32.00	5.50/ 5.50
17		12.00/12.00/ 4.00	65.50	44.00/ 44.00	6.50/ 6.50
12	+17.00	21.00/21.00/ 7.00	114.50	77.00/ 77.00	11.50/11.50
5					
34					
4					
19					
3		33.00/33.00/11.00	191.50	121.00/121.00	6.50/ 6.50
[13]	−51.00	(Artificially added!! $68.00 loss minus $17.00 ahead.)			
12 ←		(I didn't bet this. It's the number after which I restarted.)			
32					
7	−45.00	(Using double-up progression, I won $6.00 on the second bet.)			
8	−38.00	(Won $7.00 on first bet above.)			
26	−31.00				
31					
32					
15					
10	−25.50				
31					
6					

4	
7	−20.00
23	
35	
24	
30	−14.50
6	
8	−8.50
32	
17	
3	
33	
00	−2.00
16	
9	+4.00
10	+7.50
34	
18	
31	
35	
7	+11.50
28	+15.00*

*See how quickly you get well even after a *catastrophic failure* when you double up. Did you notice that after I was ahead, I reverted to the original betting scheme?

Let's look at how our spin sequences play betting the 3-3-1 variation. The bad news is that I got so angry that I threw away the paper with the spin sequence on it after the one time that I hit the wall. In fact, hitting the wall (a losing streak of nine in the case of the thrown-away note!) is what forced me to come up with the alternate plan in which you have to stop after a certain number of consecutive losses, sweat out the streak until its end, and then restart. It's also what turned me on to the Three Double-Row variation.

As you will see in the following spin sequences, there are only three losing streaks of more than six spins. That is, of course, why I recommend that your betting scheme go up to at least seven bets.

All the profits are based on the following betting scheme. Remember, I did not bet until one of the numbers hit.

Bet	*Running Total*	*Win for the Spin*	*Profit*
1.00/ 1.00/ .50	2.50		3.50/6.50
1.50/ 1.50/ .50	6.00	5.50/ 5.50	3.00/3.00
3.00/ 3.00/1.00	13.00	11.00/11.00	5.00/5.00
4.50/ 4.50/1.50	23.50	16.50/16.50	3.50/3.50
7.50/ 7.50/2.50	41.00	27.50/27.50	4.00/4.00
12.00/12.00/3.00	68.00	45.00/45.00	4.00/4.00
21.00/21.00/7.00	117.00	77.00/77.00	9.00/9.00

From this point forward, there will be only one set of numbers at the end of each sequence—the number of wins/the number of losses.

00		27	47	33	
29	3.5	6		6	
1		30	50	31	
21		22		12	98.5
11	8.5	24		5	
10	12	9	55	1	
13		22		32	
00	15	7	58	25	102
18		14		1	
27	18	36		35	
16		7	63	25	107
8	21	11	66.5	34	
17		19		28	110
16		18		5	
4		28	71.5	23	
20		16		12	115
25	25	28	74.5	23	
5		2		7	118
3		7	77.5	1	
29	30	31		8	111
19		2		1	
4		32		31	
30	35	27	81	23	
18		3		31	
0	38	8	84	30	115
33		8	87.5	7	118.5
6		24		00	125
11	43	19		33	
33		21		3	
24		35		3	
4		7	91.5	21	
5		25	95	6	

6	
3	8
29	11.5
14	
28	14.5
17	
23	
35	
26	18
33	
8	21
27	24.5
31	
16	
8	29.5
31	
22	
27	34.5
8	38
19	
11	41
3	
29	44
24	
24	
22	
21	6.5

TOTAL 46/123

7	
32	
24	
9	5
5	
19	
1	
0	8.5
22	
26	11.5
6	
7	14.5
33	
18	
16	
11	18
24	
30	21
26	24.5
13	
27	27.5
13	
17	
8	32.5
8	36
7	39.5
6	
21	
5	
10	43
8	46.5
1	

19	
7	51.5
18	
34	45.5

TOTAL 15/36

15	
24	
17	
26	
25	3.5
25	7
13	
8	10
18	
7	13
30	16.5
1	
9	19.5
11	23
8	26.5
5	
35	
7	31.5
7	35
4	
5	
6	
30	38.5
27	42
32	
7	45
4	
3	
25	50
7	53.5
12	57
4	

	20	
	7	62
	16	
	5	
	6	
	00	65.5
	25	69
TOTAL	20/39	

0	
0	6.5
0	13
15	
21	
8	18
19	
14	
14	
29	21.5
15	
12	24.5
24	
14	
00	29.5
18	
4	
7	34.5
6	
15	
35	
36	
1	
9	38.5
7	42
12	45.5
18	
19	
13	
25	49
31	
29	52
24	
16	
20	
28	55.5
28	59
9	62.5
3	
1	
30	67.5
5	65

TOTAL 17/42

36	
4	
0	
30	3.5
36	
17	
12	8.5
26	12
26	15.5
23	
20	
33	
20	
19	
11	19.5
00	26
16	
8	29
20	
0	32
00	38.5
32	
4	
35	
27	42
2	
14	
0	47
0	53.5
2	
22	
5	

	23	
	26	57.5
	10	61
	00	67.5
	00	74
	15	
	18	
	15	
	27	77.5
	15	
	27	80.5
	31	
	3	
	29	85.5
TOTAL	20/46	

19/43

22	
13	
30	
12	3.5
32	
4	
10	8.5
34	
3	
19	
00	12
7	15.5
10	
32	
18	
11	20.5
30	24
28	27.5
32	
11	30.5
12	34
12	37.5
30	41
4	
22	
24	
1	
2	
14	
00	50
1	
5	
27	55
9	58.5
14	
22	
2	
7	62
16	59.5

TOTAL 17/39

12	
7	3.5
33	
36	
3	
20	
15	
23	
21	−113.5
7	−110
15	
5	
19	
00	−106.5
25	−103
14	
36	
4	
16	
3	
5	
30	−94
6	
14	
24	
19	
14	
30	−90
1	
4	−96
TOTAL	7/30
	4/6

33	
22	
31	
11	
0	6.5
14	
11	9.5
36	
1	
21	
13	
25	13.5
2	
30	16.5
25	20
7	23.5
TOTAL	7/16

17	
2	
29	
9	3.5
25	7
32	
29	10
2	
30	13
21	
9	16
9	19.5
8	23
16	
2	
9	28
20	
18	
18	
0	31.5
5	
36	
30	36.5
35	
12	39.5
28	43
27	46.5

TOTAL 15/27

4	
36	
3	
19	
20	
10	
27	3.5
9	7
17	
35	
32	
2	
12	11
34	
1	
9	16

TOTAL 5/16

2	
9	
24	
2	
33	
9	3.5
3	
28	6.5
16	
10	9.5
5	
19	
36	
35	
25	13.5
23	
20	
3	
0	17
0	23.5
0	30
6	
14	
1	
4	
30	34
20	
7	37
28	40.5
27	44
00	50.5
3	

	3	
	15	
	11	54
	0	60.5
	8	64
	3	
	10	67.5
	32	
	14	
	15	
	24	
	15	
	10	71.5
TOTAL	18/45	

30	
31	
10	
27	3.5
19	
17	
10	8.5
0	15
2	
17	
35	
16	
12	19
25	22.5
1	
15	
0	27.5
16	
0	30.5
5	
31	
0	35.5
15	
12	38.5
00	45
00	51.5
21	
3	
1	
4	
36	
17	
9	60.5
15	
28	63.5
30	67
5	
34	61

TOTAL 15/38

8	
34	
26	3.5
33	
17	
2	
31	
18	
12	7.5
30	11
8	14..5
17	
12	17.5
5	
34	
19	
4	
3	
12	21.5
32	
7	24.5
8	28
26	31.5
31	
32	
15	
10	35
31	
6	
4	
7	38.5
23	

35	
24	
30	42
6	
8	45
32	
17	
3	
33	
00	49
16	
9	52
10	55.5
34	
18	
31	
35	
7	59.5
28	63
TOTAL	19/51

9	
12	3.5
35	
31	
12	8.5
6	
28	11.5
1	
0	14.5
3	
00	17.5
33	
16	
32	
8	21
TOTAL	7/15

16	
4	
28	
27	3.5
22	
18	
10	8.5
21	
2	
25	13.5
3	
11	16.5
14	
3	
7	21.5
2	
26	24.5
27	28
27	31.5
21	
00	34.5
5	
20	
15	
27	38
30	41.5
12	45
30	48.5
29	52
32	
11	55

TOTAL 16/31

10	
16	
1	
20	
11	3.5
5	
23	
24	
27	7
9	10.5
33	
17	
13	
18	
9	14.5
14	12

TOTAL 5/16

8	
1	
19	
0	5
23	
25	8
17	
17	
4	
33	
21	
36	
12	17
19	
8	20
7	23.5
27	27
19	
22	
11	32
12	35.5
8	39
16	
3	
0	44
19	41.5
TOTAL	11/26

9	
35	
9	3.5
20	
6	
10	8.5
34	
18	
8	13.5
12	17
31	
26	20
4	
12	23
13	
26	26
27	29.5
36	
0	32.5
20	
00	35.5
12	39
19	
24	
5	
18	
11	43
21	
26	46
10	49.5
29	53
3	

00	56
20	
7	59
35	
11	62
10	65.5
11	69
16	
0	72
24	
2	
9	77
3	
32	
7	82
13	
21	
23	
31	
12	86
10	89.5
27	93
TOTAL	27/54

9	
5	
19	
1	
0	3.5
22	
26	6.5
6	
7	9.5
33	
18	
16	
11	13
24	
30	16
26	19.5
13	
27	22.5
13	
17	
8	27.5
8	31
7	34.5
6	
21	
5	
10	38
8	41.5
1	
19	
7	46.5
18	
4	40.5

TOTAL 14/33

10	
13	
13	
35	
3	
24	
18	
4	−117
36	
2	
25	−112
13	
26	−109
18	
31	
12	−104

TOTAL 4/16

With this variation, in twenty sessions of different lengths, again there were only two losing sessions; but they were big ones—104 and 96 units. On the other hand, the eighteen winning sessions won a total of 875.5 units. Total gain was 675.5 units. I must add that once, while watching another dealer deal roulette where I work, I saw her throw thirteen losers in a row using this variation (although there were two 2s and one 3 rolled in that run)!

It was, in fact, the two losing sessions listed, the one that I threw away, and the thirteen-in-a-row that I witnessed but didn't record (I was on a work break and didn't have paper and pencil handy) that forced me to revise my thinking. I started out using this system—and still strongly like it—*if I'm using the casino's money*. But I wanted a system that would minimize losing sessions while still giving me ample return for my bets. That's when I began experimenting with the combination progressions beginning on page 00. But first let's carry our prime-number betting to its logical end by looking at two more variations.

TWO DOUBLE – ROW VARIATION

A second variation of the same theme is to bet the two 5-to-1 Double-Row bets, the 7–2 and the 25–30. As with variations, the more numbers you remove from the grouping, the less often the numbers hit and the longer the stretches between hits *can* be. In the spin sequences below, there are two losing stretches of nine and one of ten. For those with a smaller bankroll who wish to try this variation, I recommend the following bet progression (but, as you can see, it busts out when the losing stretch of ten hits):

Bet	*Running Total*	*Win for the Spin*	*Profit*
1.00/ 1.00	2.00	4.00	4.00
1.00/ 1.00	4.00	4.00	2.00
1.00/ 1.00	6.00	4.00	0
2.00/ 2.00	10.00	8.00	2.00
3.00/ 3.00	16.00	12.00	2.00
4.00/ 4.00	24.00	16.00	0
6.00/ 6.00	36.00	24.00	0
9.00/ 9.00	54.00	36.00	0
14.00/14.00	82.00	56.00	2.00
21.00/21.00	124.00	84.00	2.00

Let's look at the first line of the progression. The *Bet* column indicates that we should bet $1.00 on each of the two Double Rows, the 7–12 and the 25–30, for a *Running Total* of $2.00 bet. If either Double Row hits, our *Win for the Spin* is $4.00 ($5.00 won on the 5 to 1 Double Row that hit minus the $1.00 we lost on the Double Row that didn't hit) leaving us a *Profit* (for that particular spin) of $4.00.

If we'd missed on the first spin and hit on the second spin, our *Win for the Spin* (the second spin) would be the same, $4.00, but our *Profit* would only be $2.00 because we'd earlier lost $2.00 on the first bet of the progression.

Let's look at our example sequence and see how this variation works:

00
29 2
1
21
11 2
10 6
13
00
18
27 8
16
8 10
17
16
4
20
25 12
5
3
29 12
19
4
30 12
18
0
33
6
11 14
33
24
4
5

27 16
6
30 18
22
24
9 18
22
7 20
14
36
7 20
11 24
19
18
28 24
16
28 26
2
7 28
31
2
32
27 30
3
8 32
8 36
24
19
21
35
7 38
25 40

33
6
31
12 42
5
1
32
25 44
1
35
25 44
34
28 46
5
23
12 46
23
7 48
1
8 50
1
31
23
31
30 52
7 56
00
33
3
3
21
6

6
3
29 58
14
28 60
17
23
35
26 62
33
8 64
27 68
31
16
8 68
31
22
27 68
8 72
19
11 74
3
29 76
24
24
22
21 66

TOTAL 42/123

Not bad. How about the other spin sequences?

7	4
32	
24	
9	4
5	
19	
1	
0	
22	
26	4
6	
7	6
33	
18	
16	
11	8
24	
30	10
26	14
13	
27	16
13	
17	
8	16
8	20
7	24
6	
21	
5	
10	26
8	30
1	
19	
7	30
18	
34	26

TOTAL 14/36

15	
24	
17	
26	2
25	6
25	10
13	
8	12
18	
7	14
30	18
1	
9	20
11	24
8	28
5	
35	
7	28
7	32
4	
5	
6	
30	34
27	38
32	
7	40
4	
3	
25	40
7	44
12	48
4	
20	
7	48
16	
5	
6	
00	
25	50

TOTAL 19/39

0	
0	
0	
15	
21	
8	0
19	
14	
14	
29	2
15	
12	4
24	
14	
00	
18	
4	
7	4
6	
15	
35	
36	
1	
9	4
7	8
12	12
18	
19	
13	
25	14
31	
29	16

	24	
	16	
	20	
	28	18
	28	22
	9	26
	3	
	1	
	30	26
	5	24
TOTAL	13/42	

36	
4	
0	
30	2
36	
17	
12	2
26	6
26	10
23	
20	
33	
20	
19	
11	10
00	
16	
8	10
20	
0	
00	
32	
4	
35	
27	10
2	
14	
0	
0	
2	
22	
5	

	23	
	26	12
	10	16
	00	
	00	
	15	
	18	
	15	
	27	16
	15	
	27	18
	31	
	3	
	29	18
TOTAL	12/46	

22	
13	
30	0
12	4
32	
4	
10	4
34	
3	
19	
00	
7	6
10	
32	
18	
11	6
30	10
28	14
32	
11	16
12	20
12	24
30	28
4	
22	
24	
1	
2	
14	
00	
1	
5	

	27	30
	9	34
	14	
	22	
	2	
	7	36
	16	34
TOTAL	15/39	

	12	3
	7	6
	33	3
	36	0
	3	4
	20	1
	15	−2
	23	−5
	21	−11
	7	1
	15	−2
	5	−5
	19	−8
	00	0
	25	3
	14	0
	36	−3
	4	−6
	16	−12
	3	4
	5	1
	30	4
	6	1
	14	−2
	24	−5
	19	−11
	14	−23
	30	−5
	1	−1
	4	−4
TOTAL	6/30	

33	
22	
31	
11	2
0	
14	
11	2
36	
1	
21	
13	
25	4
2	
30	6
25	10
7	14

TOTAL 6/16

7	4
2	
29	6
9	10
25	14
32	
29	16
2	
30	18
21	
9	20
9	24
8	28
16	
2	
9	28
20	
18	
18	
0	
5	
36	
30	28
35	
12	30
28	34
27	38

TOTAL 14/27

4	
36	
3	
19	
20	
10	0
27	4
9	8
17	
35	
32	
2	
12	10
34	
1	
9	10
TOTAL 5/16	

2	
9	2
24	
2	
33	
9	4
3	
28	6
16	
10	8
5	
19	
36	
35	
25	10
23	
20	
3	
0	
0	
0	
6	
14	
1	
4	−114
30	−112
20	
7	−110
28	−106
27	−102
00	
3	

3	
15	
11	−100
0	
8	−98
3	
10	−96
32	
14	
15	
24	
15	
10	−96
TOTAL 13/45	

30	4
31	
10	6
27	10
19	
17	
10	10
0	
2	
17	
35	
16	
12	10
25	14
1	
15	
0	
16	
0	
5	
31	
0	
15	
12	16
00	
00	
21	
3	
1	
4	
36	
17	

	9	18
	15	
	28	20
	30	24
	5	
	34	20
TOTAL	10/38	

8	4
34	
26	6
33	
17	
2	
31	
18	
12	6
30	10
8	14
17	
12	16
5	
34	
19	
4	
3	
12	16
32	
7	18
8	22
26	26
31	
32	
15	
10	28
31	
6	
4	
7	30
23	

35	
24	
30	32
6	
8	34
32	
17	
3	
33	
00	
16	
9	34
10	38
34	
18	
31	
35	
7	40
28	44

TOTAL 18/51

9	4
12	8
35	
31	
12	8
6	
28	10
1	
0	
3	
00	
33	
16	
32	
8	10

TOTAL 5/15

16	
4	
28	0
27	4
22	
18	
10	4
21	
2	
25	4
3	
11	6
14	
3	
7	6
2	
26	8
27	12
27	16
21	
00	
5	
20	
15	
27	16
30	20
12	24
30	28
29	32
32	
11	34

TOTAL 15/31

	10	4
	16	
	1	
	20	
	11	6
	5	
	23	
	24	
	27	8
	9	12
	33	
	17	
	13	
	18	
	9	14
	14	12
TOTAL	5/16	

	8	4
	1	
	19	
	0	
	23	
	25	6
	17	
	17	
	4	
	33	
	21	
	36	
	12	6
	19	
	8	8
	7	12
	27	16
	19	
	22	
	11	16
	12	20
	8	24
	16	
	3	
	0	
	19	14
TOTAL	9/26	

29	4
35	
9	6
20	
6	
10	6
34	
18	
8	6
12	10
31	
26	12
4	
12	14
13	
26	16
27	20
36	
0	
20	
00	
12	22
19	
24	
5	
18	
11	24
21	
26	26
10	30
29	34
3	

	00	
	20	
	7	36
	35	
	11	38
	10	42
	11	46
	16	
	0	
	24	
	2	
	9	48
	3	
	32	
	7	48
	13	
	21	
	23	
	31	
	12	50
	10	54
	27	58
TOTAL	23/54	

9	4
5	
19	
1	
0	
22	
26	4
6	
7	6
33	
18	
16	
11	8
24	
30	10
26	14
13	
27	16
13	
17	
8	16
8	20
7	24
6	
21	
5	
10	26
8	30
1	
19	
7	30
18	

4	26

TOTAL 13/33

10	4
13	
13	
35	
3	
24	
18	
4	
36	
2	
25	6
13	
26	8
18	
31	
12	8

TOTAL 4/16

Again, in twenty sessions we have eighteen winners and only two losers. The winners total 508 units, the losers one hundred, for a total gain of four hundred and eight. Not too shabby. But look, again we suffer one big losing session. If you can afford one big loser, give this run a try.

ONE DOUBLE-ROW VARIATION

I knew you'd ask yourself, "What happens if you bet only one Double-Row?" Here it is. You'll notice that there are numerous long losing stretches. In the spin sequences I experienced, the longest losing streak was twenty! To make matters worse, you risk more than the $69 our primary system bets for significantly less gain. I won't detail all the particulars; suffice it to say I don't recommend wasting time with this variation. I'll just give you the figures so you can satisfy your curiosity.

I'll use the following betting progression. It covers twenty bets:

Bet	*Running Total*	*Win for the Spin*	*Profit*
1.00	1.00	5.00	5.00
1.00	2.00	5.00	4.00
1.00	3.00	5.00	3.00
1.00	4.00	5.00	2.00
1.00	5.00	5.00	1.00
1.50	6.50	7.50	2.50
1.50	8.00	7.50	1.00
2.00	10.00	10.00	2.00
2.00	12.00	10.00	0
2.50	14.50	12.50	.50
3.00	17.50	15.00	.50

3.50	21.00	17.50	0
4.50	25.50	22.50	1.50
5.50	31.00	27.50	2.00
6.50	37.50	32.50	1.50
7.50	45.00	37.50	0
9.00	54.00	45.00	0
11.00	65.00	55.00	1.00
13.00	78.00	65.00	0
16.00	94.00	80.00	2.00

How does our base sequence look?

00		4		21	
29		5		35	
1		27		7	30.5
21		6		25	
11	1	30		33	
10	6	22		6	
13		24		31	
00		9	9	12	31.5
18		22		5	
27		7	13	1	
16		14		32	
8	8.5	36		25	
17		7	16	1	
16		11	21	35	
4		19		25	
20		18		34	
25		28		28	
5		16		5	
3		28		23	
29		2		12	31.5
19		7	22	23	
4		31		7	35.5
30		2		1	
18		32		8	39.5
0		27		1	
33		3		31	
6		8	24.5	23	
11	8.5	8	29.5	31	
33		24		30	
24		19		7	42

00
33
3
3
21
6
6
3
29
14
28
17
23
35
26
33
8 42
27
31
16
8 44
31
22
27
8 46
19
11 50
3
29
24
24

22
21 43.5

TOTAL 21/123

What about the other spin sequences?

7	5
32	
24	
9	8
5	
19	
1	
0	
22	
26	
6	
7	10
33	
18	
16	
11	12
24	
30	
26	
13	
27	
13	
17	
8	14
8	19
7	24
6	
21	
5	
10	26
8	31
1	
19	
7	34
18	
34	32

TOTAL 10/36

15	
24	
17	
26	
25	
25	
13	
8	2
18	
7	6
30	
1	
9	9
11	14
8	19
5	
35	
7	22
7	27
4	
5	
6	
30	
27	
32	
7	28
4	
3	
25	
7	30
12	35
4	
20	
7	38
16	
5	
6	
00	
25	33

TOTAL 11/39

70	
0	
0	
15	
21	
8	2.5
19	
14	
14	
29	
15	
12	5
24	
14	
00	
18	
4	
7	7.5
6	
15	
35	
36	
1	
9	10
7	15
12	20
18	
19	
13	
25	
31	
29	

	24	
	16	
	20	
	28	
	28	
	9	20
	3	
	1	
	30	
	5	16
TOTAL	7/42	

36	
4	
0	
30	
36	
17	
12	1
26	
26	
23	
20	
33	
20	
19	
11	3
00	
16	
8	6
20	
0	
00	
32	
4	
35	
27	
2	
14	
0	
0	
2	
22	
5	
23	
26	
10	6
00	
00	
15	
18	
15	
27	
15	
27	
31	
3	
29	−11.5

TOTAL 4/46

22	
13	
30	
12	2
32	
4	
10	7
34	
3	
19	
00	
7	8
10	13
32	
18	
11	16
30	
28	
32	
11	18
12	23
12	28
30	
4	
22	
24	
1	
2	
14	
00	
1	
5	

	27	
	9	28
	14	
	22	
	2	
	7	30
	16	29
TOTAL	10/39	

12	5
7	10
33	
36	
3	
20	
15	
23	
21	
7	12
15	
5	
19	
00	
25	
14	
36	
4	
16	
3	
5	
30	
6	
14	
24	
19	
14	
30	
1	
4	−84

TOTAL 3/30

33	
22	
31	
11	2
0	
14	
11	5
36	
1	
21	
13	
25	
2	
30	
25	
7	5

TOTAL 3/16

	7	5
	2	
	29	
	9	8
	25	
	32	
	29	
	2	
	30	
	21	
	9	9
	9	14
	8	19
	16	
	2	
	9	22
	20	
	18	
	18	
	0	
	5	
	36	
	30	
	35	
	12	22
	28	
	27	20
TOTAL	7/27	

	4	
	36	
	3	
	19	
	20	
	10	2.5
	27	
	9	6.5
	17	
	35	
	32	
	2	
	12	7.5
	34	
	1	
	9	10.5
TOTAL	4/16	

2	
9	4
24	
2	
33	
9	6
3	
28	
16	
10	8
5	
19	
36	
35	
25	
23	
20	
3	
0	
0	
0	
6	
14	
1	
4	
30	
20	
7	12
28	
27	
00	
3	

	3	
	15	
	11	13
	0	
	8	17
	3	
	10	21
	32	
	14	
	15	
	24	
	15	
	10	23.5
TOTAL	8/45	

30	
31	
10	3
27	
19	
17	
10	5
0	
2	
17	
35	
16	
12	7.5
25	
1	
15	
0	
16	
0	
5	
31	
0	
15	
12	8
00	
00	
21	
3	
1	
4	
36	
17	

	9	8
	15	
	28	
	30	
	5	
	34	3
TOTAL	5/38	

8 5
34
26
33
17
2
31
18
12 7
30
8 11
17
12 15
5
34
19
4
3
12 17.5
32
7 21.5
8 26.5
26
31
32
15
10 27.5
31
6
4
7 29.5
23

35
24
30
6
8 32
32
17
3
33
00
16
9 33
10 38
34
18
31
35
7 39
28 38

TOTAL 13/51

	9	5
	12	10
	35	
	31	
	12	13
	6	
	28	
	1	
	0	
	3	
	00	
	33	
	16	
	32	
	8	13.5
TOTAL	4/15	

	16	
	4	
	28	
	27	
	22	
	18	
	10	1
	21	
	2	
	25	
	3	
	11	2
	14	
	3	
	7	5
	2	
	26	
	27	
	27	
	21	
	00	
	5	
	20	
	15	
	27	
	30	
	12	5
	30	
	29	
	32	
	11	7
TOTAL	5/31	

10	5
16	
1	
20	
11	7
5	
23	
24	
27	
9	8
33	
17	
13	
18	
9	9
14	8
TOTAL	4/16

8	5
1	
19	
0	
23	
25	
17	
17	
4	
33	
21	
36	
12	5
19	
8	9
7	14
27	
19	
22	
11	16
12	21
8	26
16	
3	
0	
19	22
TOTAL	7/26

29	
35	
9	3
20	
6	
10	6
34	
18	
8	9
12	14
31	
26	
4	
12	16
13	
26	
27	
36	
0	
20	
00	
12	18
19	
24	
5	
18	
11	19
21	
26	
10	22
29	
3	

00	
20	
7	23
35	
11	27
10	32
11	37
16	
0	
24	
2	
9	38
3	
32	
7	41
13	
21	
23	
31	
12	42
10	47
27	46

TOTAL 16/54

9 5
5
19
1
0
22
26
6
7 7
33
18
16
11 9
24
30
26
13
27
13
17
8 11
8 16
7 21
6
21
5
10 23
8 28
1
19
7 31
18
4 29

TOTAL 9/33

10 5
13
13
35
3
24
18
4
36
2
25
13
26
18
31
12 5.5

TOTAL 2/16

Par for the course. We suffer two losing sessions in twenty. But again, one of the sessions is a big loser—84 units. The other loser is 11.5, bringing total losses to 95.5. On the plus side, the eighteen times we win we earn 383.5 units. Total gain is 284 units. This is 60 less than the 344 we gain using our basic Three Double-Row system while risking more money. Why play it?

6

Combinations

Only you know the bankroll you have available. Personally (and I will repeat this later), I like to take more risks with the house's money than with my own. With this in mind, let's look at some more variations based on a combination of the above systems. As always, the more numbers we cover initially, the larger our bet must be and, consequently, the faster our progression accelerates; but—on the flip side—the fewer numbers we cover initially, the less we risk and the more slowly our progression accelerates. The following three progressions are based on tactics used by gunners in the military. In the first progression, we'll start with a smaller target area, expand it as we contnue to miss the target, then reduce it again when we're *running low on ammunition* (defined as either risking a larger amount of money or approaching the table maximum).

In this progression, with our first three bets we cover only the numbers 7 through 12 and 25 through 30—the core numbers of all the variations in this book. After three misses we expand our target area to include the 0 and 00 for two spins.

Then, for the next three spins we include the 1, 2, and 3. If we haven't hit after eight spins (because we're running low on ammo), we reduce our target area back down to the 7 through 12 and 25 through 30. I've designed this progression to be played on a dime ($.10) roulette table to lower the initial bankroll we risk. There are several dime roulette tables in the Las Vegas area. For those readers in other parts of the country, if you can't find a dime table, just double all the figures and bet it on a quarter ($.25) table.

(For the following three variations, I will carry the progression out to the point where you would reach the table maximum.)

Don't panic at this, however, because none of the spin sequences in this book even approach this level of betting. But you never really know—this *is* gambling. A player once told me he was at the Stardust Hotel and Casino in Las Vegas and saw the number 6 hit five times in a row. The 6, of course, is not one of our numbers—it would take only two more misses to blow our .50-.50-.50-1.00-2.00 . . . progression out of the water. So, I think it only fair to continue the progression until the table maximum is reached. In these tables, the Win for the Spin is eliminated to fit the page.

Bet	*Target Area*	*Total Bet*	*Profit*
.25/.25	7–12,25–30	.50	1.00/1.00
.25/.25	7–12,25–30	1.00	.50/.50
.25/.25	7–12,25–30	1.50	0/0
.50/.50/.25	7–12,25–30,0–00	2.75	.25/1.75
.75/.75/.25	7–12,25–30,0–00	4.50	0/0
1.50/1.50/1.25	7–12,25–30,0–3	8.75	.25/0

3.00/3.00/2.50	7–12,25–30,0–3	17.25	.75/.25
5.50/5.50/4.75	7–12,25–30,0–3	33.00	0/.25
8.25/8.25	7–12,25–30	49.50	0/0
12.50/12.50	7–12,25–30	74.50	.50/.50
18.50/18.50	7–12,25–30	111.50	–.50/–.50
28.00/28.00	7–12,25–30	167.50	.50/.50
40.00/40.00	7–12,25–30	247.50	–7.50/–7.50

There you have it—our first combination progression. By now, I hope you understand what I mean by the target area. If not, I'll reiterate: 7–12 or 25–30 means betting the 7–12 or 25–30 Double Rows; 0-00 means betting the 0-00 Split; 0-3 means betting the 0-3 Special Double Row. Again, don't worry about such things as losing $7.50 on *the thirteenth bet!!* I've only included it to carry the progression to its end—reaching the table limit. You'll see in the spin sequences that you don't even get close to a thirteenth spin. Also, although we're betting quarters at the beginning, you can't bet this on a quarter table because on a quarter table the minimum inside bet is normally $1.00. On dime tables the minimum is $.50.

Now let's look at the spin sequences, with the running win total to the right:

00
29 .50
1
21
11 .50
10 1.50
13
00
18
27 1.75
16
8 2.25
17
16
4
20
25 2.25
5
3
29
19
4
30
18
0
33
6
11 2.25
33
24
4
5

27 2.25
6
30 2.75
22
24
9 2.75
22
7 3.25
14
36
7 3.25
11 4.25
27 5.25
19
18
28 5.25
16
28 5.75
2
7 6.25
31
2
32
27 6.50
3
8 7.00
8 8.00
24
19
21
35
7 8.00

25 9.00
33
6
31
12 9.25
5
1
32
25 9.50
1
35
25 9.50
34
28 10.00
5
23
12 10.00
23
7 10.50
1
8 11.00
1
31
23
31
30 11.00
7 12.00
00
33
3
3
21

6
3 12.25
9 13.25
14
28 13.75
17
23
35
26 14.00
33
8 14.50
27 15.50
31
16
8 15.50
31
22
27 15.50
8 16.50
19
11
3
29 16.75
24
24
22
21

TOTAL 43/123

7 1.00
32
24
9 1.00
5
19
1
0 2.75
22
26 3.25
6
7 3.75
33
18
16
11 4.00
24
30 4.50
26 5.50
13
27 6.00
13
17
8 6.00
8 7.00
7 8.00
6
21
5
10 8.25
8 9.25
1
19
7 9.25
18
4

TOTAL 15/36

15	
24	
17	
26	.25
25	1.25
25	2.25
13	
8	2.75
18	
7	3.25
30	4.25
1	
9	4.75
11	5.75
8	6.75
5	
35	
7	6.75
7	7.75
4	
5	
6	
30	8.00
27	9.00
32	
7	9.50
4	
3	
25	9.50
7	10.50
12	11.50
4	
20	
7	11.50
16	
5	
6	
00	13.25
25	14.25

TOTAL 20/39

0	
0	
0	
15	
21	
8	.25
19	
14	
14	
29	.50
15	
12	1.00
24	
14	
00	
18	
4	
7	1.25
6	
15	
35	
36	
1	
9	1.50
7	2.50
12	3.50
18	
19	
13	
25	3.75
31	
29	4.25

	24	
	16	
	20	
	28	4.50
	28	5.50
	9	6.50
	3	
	1	
	30	6.50
	5	
TOTAL	13/42	

36	
4	
0	
30	.25
36	
17	
12	.25
26	1.25
26	2.25
23	
20	
33	
20	
19	
11	2.50
00	
16	
8	2.50
20	
0	
00	
32	
4	
35	
27	3.25
2	
14	
0	
0	5.00
2	
22	
5	

	23	
	26	5.00
	10	6.00
	00	
	00	
	15	
	18	
	15	
	27	6.25
	15	
	27	6.75
	31	
	3	
	29	6.75
TOTAL	13/46	

22	
13	
30	.00
12	1.00
32	
4	
10	1.00
34	
3	
19	
00	2.75
7	3.75
10	4.75
32	
18	
11	4.75
30	5.75
28	6.75
32	
11	7.25
12	8.25
12	9.25
30	10.25
4	
22	
24	
1	
2	
14	
00	10.00
1	
5	
27	10.00
9	11.00
14	
22	
2	
7	11.25

TOTAL 17/38

12	1.00
7	2.00
33	
36	
3	
20	
15	
23	
21	
7	2.00
15	
5	
19	
00	3.75
25	4.75
14	
36	
4	
16	
3	
5	
30	5.50
6	
14	
24	
19	
14	
30	5.75
1	
4	
TOTAL	7/30

33	
22	
31	
11	.25
0	
14	
11	.25
36	
1	
21	
13	
25	.25
2	
30	.75
25	1.75
7	2.75
TOTAL	6/16

7	1.00
2	
29	1.50
9	2.50
25	3.50
32	
29	4.00
2	
30	4.50
21	
9	5.00
9	6.00
8	7.00
16	
2	
9	7.00
20	
18	
18	
0	7.75
5	
36	
30	7.75
35	
12	8.25
28	9.25
27	10.25

TOTAL 15/27

4	
36	
3	
19	
20	
10	.25
27	1.25
9	2.25
17	
35	
32	
2	
12	2.25
34	
1	
9	2.25

TOTAL 5/16

2
9 .50
24
2
33
9 .75
3
28 1.25
16
10 1.75
5
19
36
35
25 1.75
23
20
3
0 3.50
0
0
6
14
1
4
30 4.25
20
7 4.75
28 5.75
27 6.75
00
3

3
15
11 6.75
0
8 7.25
3
10 7.75
32
14
15
24
15
10 8.00

TOTAL 14/45

30	1.00
31	
10	1.50
27	2.50
19	
17	
10	2.50
0	
2	
17	
35	
16	
12	2.75
25	3.75
1	
15	
0	
16	
0	3.75
5	
31	
0	
15	
12	3.75
00	
00	
21	
3	
1	
4	
36	
17	

	9	3.75
	15	
	28	4.25
	30	5.25
	5	
	34	
TOTAL	11/39	

8	1.00
34	
26	1.50
33	
17	
2	
31	
18	
12	1.75
30	2.75
8	3.75
17	
12	4.25
5	
34	
19	
4	
3	
12	4.50
32	
7	5.00
8	6.00
26	7.00
31	
32	
15	
10	7.25
31	
6	
4	
7	7.50
23	

35	
24	
30	7.75
6	
8	8.25
32	
17	
3	
33	
00	8.25
16	
9	8.75
10	9.75
34	
18	
31	
35	
7	9.75
28	10.75

TOTAL 19/51

9	1.00
12	2.00
35	
31	
12	2.00
6	
28	2.50
1	
0	
3	
00	4.25
33	
16	
32	
8	4.50

TOTAL 6/15

16	
4	
28	0
27	1.00
22	
18	
10	1.00
21	
2	
25	1.00
3	
11	1.50
14	
3	
7	1.50
2	
26	2.00
27	3.00
27	4.00
21	
00	
5	
20	
15	
27	4.25
30	5.25
12	6.25
30	7.25
29	8.25
32	
11	8.75

TOTAL 15/31

10	.50
16	1.00
1	1.75
20	2.25
11	2.75
5	
23	
24	
27	3.25
9	3.75
33	
17	3.75
13	
18	3.75
9	4.25
14	

TOTAL 5/16

8	1.00
1	
19	
0	
23	
25	1.00
17	
17	
4	
33	
21	
36	
12	1.75
19	
8	2.25
7	3.25
27	4.25
19	
22	
11	4.75
12	5.75
8	6.75
16	
1	
0	
19	

TOTAL 9/26

29	1.00
35	
9	1.50
20	
6	
10	1.50
34	
18	
8	1.50
12	2.50
31	
26	3.00
4	
12	3.50
13	
26	4.00
27	5.00
36	
0	
20	
00	5.25
12	6.25
19	
24	
5	
18	
11	6.25
21	
26	6.75
10	7.75
29	8.75
3	
00	
20	
7	9.00
35	
11	9.50
10	10.50
11	11.50
16	
0	
24	
2	
9	11.50
3	
32	
7	11.50
13	
21	
23	
31	
12	11.50
10	12.50
27	13.50

TOTAL 24/54

<u>9</u>	1.00
5	
19	
1	
<u>0</u>	2.75
22	
<u>26</u>	3.25
6	
<u>7</u>	4.00
33	
18	
16	
<u>11</u>	4.25
24	
<u>30</u>	4.75
<u>26</u>	5.75
13	
<u>27</u>	6.25
13	
17	
<u>8</u>	6.25
<u>8</u>	7.25
<u>7</u>	8.25
6	
21	
5	
<u>10</u>	8.50
<u>8</u>	9.50
1	
19	
<u>7</u>	10.50
18	
4	

TOTAL 14/33

<u>10</u>	.50
13	
13	
35	
3	1.50
24	
18	1.50
4	
36	
<u>2</u>	2.00
<u>25</u>	2.50
13	
<u>26</u>	2.50
18	3.00
31	
<u>12</u>	3.00

TOTAL 5/16

As I said, we don't even approach fourteen losses in a row. The most we lose in a row is nine—and that twice. Looking back at our progression, that means we would risk $74.50 twice. How about the results? We net 276 hits out of 39 spins. That's better than a 37 percent win rate! As for units—assuming our unit is $.25, we've just won $161.00 while risking at the most $74.50. Our gain is better than double our risk!

Don't forget, if you can't find a dime roulette table, just double all the figures and find a quarter table.

Now let's look at almost a reversal of the above progression, starting out with a large target area and continually reducing it until we hit a prime number (a 7–12 or a 25–30). Since we are starting with a larger target area, we can't use this progression on a dime table, we must use it on a quarter table. Most quarter tables start with a minimum of $1.00 inside and end with $1,000.00 maximum payoff per individual bet, so our progression will start with a dollar and go until we reach the table maximum. (Again, no need to panic. We don't get near the table maximum.)

With this particular progression, we are going to add *one time* a fourth Double Row bet. I prefer the 16–21 Double Row because of the arrangement of the numbers on the wheel.

Bear in mind that starting with a larger initial bet accelerates this progression rapidly.

Bet	*Target Area*	*Total Bet*	*Profit*
.25/.25/.25/.25	7–12,16–21, 25–30,0–3	1.00	.50/.50/.50/.75
.50/.50/.50	7–12,25–30,0–3	2.50	.50/.50/1.00
1.00/1.00/.75	7–12,25–30,0–3	5.25	.75/.75/0
1.75/1.75/1.50	7–12,25–30,0–3	10.25	.50/.50/.25
3.25/3.25/2.75	7–12,25–30,0–3	19.50	0/0/–.25
6.25/6.25/5.50	7–12,25–30,0–3	37.50	0/0/1.00

Bet	*Target Area*	*Total Bet*	*Profit*
10.50/10.50/3.50	7–12,25–30,0–00	52.00	1.00/1.00/1.00
15.00/15.00/5.00	7–12,25–30,0–00	87.00	3.00/3.00/3.00
22.00/22.00	7–12,25–30	133.00	1.00/1.00/1.00
34.00/34.00	7–12,25–30	201.00	3.00/3.00/3.00
50.00/50.00	7–12,25–30	301.00	−1.00/−1.00/−1.00
75.00/75.00	7–12,25–30	451.00	−1.00/−1.00/−1.00
113.00/113.00	7–12,25–30	677.00	1.00/1.00/1.00
170.00/170.00	7–12,25–30	917.00	3.00/3.00/3.00

A total bet of $917.00! Mr. Smart, are you out of your mind? No, I'm not. Let's look at the spin sequences before we panic.

00	.75
29	1.25
1	2.00
21	2.50
11	3.00
10	3.50
13	
00	4.50
18	5.00
27	5.50
16	6.00
8	6.50
17	7.00
16	7.50
4	
20	
25	8.25
5	
3	9.25
29	9.75
19	10.25
4	
30	10.75
18	11.25
0	12.00
33	
6	
11	12.75
33	
24	
4	
5	

27	12.75
6	
30	13.25
22	
24	
9	14.00
22	
7	14.50
14	
36	
7	15.25
11	15.75
27	16.25
19	16.75
18	17.25
28	17.75
16	18.25
28	18.75
2	19.50
7	20.00
31	
2	21.00
32	
27	21.50
3	22.25
8	22.75
8	23.25
24	
19	
21	
35	
7	23.25

25	23.75
33	
6	
31	
12	24.25
5	
1	25.25
32	
25	25.75
1	26.50
35	
25	27.00
34	
28	27.50
5	
23	
12	28.25
23	
7	28.75
1	29.50
8	30.00
1	30.75
31	
23	
31	
30	31.25
7	31.75
00	32.50
33	
3	33.50
3	34.25
21	34.75

	6	
	6	
	3	34.75
	9	35.25
	14	
	28	35.75
	17	36.25
	23	
	35	
	26	37.00
	33	
	8	37.50
	27	38.00
	31	
	16	
	8	38.75
	31	
	22	
	27	39.50
	8	40.00
	19	40.50
	11	41.00
	3	41.75
	29	42.25
	24	
	24	
	22	
	21	
TOTAL	73/123	

7	.50
32	
24	
9	1.25
5	
19	
1	1.25
0	2.00
22	
26	2.50
6	
7	3.00
33	
18	
16	
11	3.50
24	
30	4.00
26	4.50
13	
27	5.00
13	
17	
8	5.75
8	6.50
7	7.25
6	
21	
5	
10	8.00
8	8.50
1	9.25

	19	9.75
	7	10.25
	18	10.75
	4	
TOTAL	19/36	

15	
24	
17	
26	.50
25	1.00
25	1.50
13	
8	2.00
18	2.50
7	3.00
30	3.50
1	4.25
9	4.75
11	5.25
8	5.75
5	
35	
7	6.50
7	7.00
4	
5	
6	
30	7.50
27	8.00
32	
7	8.50
4	
3	9.50
25	10.00
7	10.50
12	11.00
4	
20	
7	11.75
16	12.25
5	
6	
00	12.25
25	12.75

TOTAL 24/39

0 .75
0 1.50
0 2.25
15
21
8 3.00
19 3.50
14
14
29 4.25
15
12 4.75
24
14
00 4.75
18 5.25
4
7 5.75
6
15
35
36
1 5.50
9 6.00
7 6.50
12 7.00
18 7.50
19 8.00
13
25 8.50
31
29 9.00
24
16
20
28 9.50
28 10.00
9 10.50
3 11.25
1 12.00
30 12.50
5

TOTAL 24/42

36	
4	
0	0
30	.50
36	
17	
12	1.25
26	1.75
26	2.25
23	
20	
33	
20	
19	
11	2.25
00	3.00
16	3.50
8	4.00
20	4.50
0	5.25
00	6.00
32	
4	
35	
27	6.50
2	7.25
14	
0	8.25
0	9.00
2	9.75
22	
5	
23	
26	10.25
10	10.75
00	11.50
00	12.25
15	
18	
15	
27	12.75
15	
27	13.25
31	
3	14.25
29	14.75

TOTAL 25/46

22	
13	
30	.50
12	1.00
32	
4	
10	1.75
34	
3	2.75
19	3.25
00	4.00
7	4.50
10	5.00
32	
18	
11	5.75
30	6.25
28	6.75
32	
11	7.25
12	7.75
12	8.25
30	8.75
4	
22	
24	
1	10.00
2	10.75
14	
00	11.75
1	12.50
5	
27	13.00
9	13.50
14	
22	
2	13.50
7	14.00

TOTAL 23/38

12	.50
7	1.00
33	
36	
3	1.00
20	1.50
15	
23	
21	
7	2.00
15	
5	
19	
00	2.25
25	2.75
14	
36	
4	
16	
3	2.50
5	
30	3.00
6	
14	
24	
19	
14	
30	3.00
1	3.75
4	

TOTAL 11/30

33	
22	
31	
11	.50
0	1.25
14	
11	1.75
36	
1	2.75
21	3.25
13	
25	3.75
2	4.50
30	5.00
25	5.50
7	6.00

TOTAL 10/16

7	.50
2	1.25
29	1.75
9	2.25
25	2.75
32	
29	3.25
2	4.00
30	4.50
21	5.00
9	5.50
9	6.00
8	6.50
16	7.00
2	7.75
9	8.25
20	8.75
18	9.25
18	9.75
0	10.50
5	
36	
30	11.25
35	
12	11.75
28	12.25
27	12.75

TOTAL 23/27

4	
36	
3	.75
19	1.25
20	1.75
10	2.25
27	2.75
9	3.25
17	3.75
35	
32	
2	3.75
12	4.25
34	
1	5.25
9	5.75

TOTAL 11/16

2	.75
9	1.25
24	
2	2.25
33	
9	2.75
3	3.50
28	4.00
16	4.50
10	5.00
5	
19	
36	
35	
25	5.00
23	
20	
3	5.00
0	5.75
0	6.50
0	7.25
6	
14	
1	7.25
4	
30	7.75
20	8.25
7	8.75
28	9.25
27	9.75
00	10.50
3	11.25
3	12.00
15	
11	12.50
0	13.25
8	13.75
3	14.50
10	15.00
32	
14	
15	
24	
15	
10	15.00

TOTAL 28/45

30	.50
31	
10	1.00
27	1.50
19	2.00
17	2.50
10	3.00
0	3.75
2	4.50
17	5.00
35	
16	
12	5.75
25	6.25
1	7.00
15	
0	8.00
16	8.50
0	9.25
5	
31	
0	9.25
15	
12	9.75
00	10.50
00	11.25
21	11.75
3	12.50
1	13.25
4	
36	
17	
9	13.75
15	
28	14.25
30	14.75
5	
34	

TOTAL 25/38

8	.50
34	
26	1.00
33	
17	
2	1.00
31	
18	
12	1.75
30	2.25
8	2.75
17	3.25
12	3.75
5	
34	
19	
4	
3	3.50
12	4.00
32	
7	4.50
8	5.00
26	5.50
31	
32	
15	
10	6.00
31	
6	
4	
7	6.50
23	

35	
24	
30	7.00
6	
8	7.50
32	
17	
3	7.50
33	
00	8.50
16	9.00
9	9.50
10	10.00
34	
18	
31	
35	
7	10.00
28	10.50

TOTAL 24/51

9	.50
12	1.00
35	
31	
12	1.75
6	
28	2.25
1	3.00
0	3.75
3	4.50
00	5.25
33	
16	
32	
8	5.75

TOTAL 9/15

16	.50
4	
28	1.00
27	1.50
22	
18	
10	2.25
21	2.75
2	3.50
25	
3	4.50
11	5.00
14	
3	6.00
7	6.50
2	7.25
26	7.75
27	8.25
27	8.75
21	9.25
00	10.00
5	
20	
15	
27	10.50
30	11.00
12	11.50
30	12.00
29	12.50
32	
11	13.00

TOTAL 22/31

10	.50
16	1.00
1	1.75
20	2.25
11	2.75
5	
23	
24	
27	3.25
9	3.75
33	
17	
13	
18	
9	3.75
14	

TOTAL 8/16

8	.50
1	1.25
19	1.75
0	2.50
23	
25	3.00
17	3.50
17	4.00
4	
33	
21	
36	
12	4.00
19	4.50
8	5.00
7	5.50
27	6.00
19	6.50
22	
11	7.00
12	7.50
8	8.00
16	8.50
1	9.25
0	10.00
19	10.50

TOTAL 20/26

29	.50
35	
9	1.00
20	1.50
6	
10	2.00
34	
18	
8	2.75
12	3.25
31	
26	3.75
4	
12	4.25
13	
26	4.75
27	5.25
36	
0	6.25
20	6.75
00	7.50
12	8.00
19	8.50
24	
5	
18	
11	9.00
21	9.50
26	10.00
10	10.50
29	11.00
3	11.75

00	12.50
20	13.00
7	13.50
35	
11	14.00
10	14.50
11	15.00
16	15.50
0	16.25
24	
2	17.25
9	17.75
3	18.50
32	
7	19.00
13	
21	
23	
31	
12	19.00
10	19.50
27	20.00

TOTAL 36/54

9	.50
5	
19	
1	.50
0	1.25
22	
26	1.75
6	
7	2.25
33	
18	
16	
11	2.75
24	
30	3.25
26	3.75
13	
27	4.25
13	
17	
8	5.00
8	5.50
7	6.00
6	
21	
5	
10	6.50
8	7.00
1	7.75
19	8.25
7	8.75
18	9.25
4	

TOTAL 18/33

10	.50
13	
13	
35	
3	.75
24	
18	
4	
36	
2	.50
25	1.00
13	
26	1.50
18	2.00
31	
12	2.50

TOTAL 7/16

The longest losing stretch is only five. But don't forget the five 6s in a row at the Stardust. I'd feel safe having enough money to make 10 bets on this progression—you'd need $201.00 for ten bets.

We can't forget the results. What are they? With this progression we win 443 out of 739 spins—almost 60 percent. If the unit is quarters, you've just won $240.25.

If you can find a dime table, here's an example of a progression you can bet on it:

Bet	*Target Area*	*Total Bet*	*Profit*
.20/.20/.20/.10	7–12,16–21,25–30,0–3	.70	.50/.50/.50/0
.30/.30/.20	7–12,25–30,0–3	1.50	.30/.30/–.10
.50/.50/.50	7–12,25–30,0–3	3.00	0/0/.50
1.00/1.00/.90	7–12,25–30,0–3	5.90	.10/.10/.40
1.90/1.90/1.70	7–12,25–30,0–3	11.40	0/0/.50
3.70/3.70/3.20	7–12,25–30,0–3	22.00	.20/.20/.40
6.00/6.00/2.00	7–12,25–30,0–00	36.00	0/0/0
11.50/11.50/9.80	7–12,25–30,0–00	68.80	.20/.20/.40
17.50/17.50	7–12,25–30	103.80	1.20/1.20
26.00/26.00	7–12,25–30	155.80	.20/.20
40.00/40.00*	7–12,25–30	235.80	4.20/4.20

*This progression assumes the table maximum is $200.00. There are dime tables with a $350.00 maximum. The following progression (carried to its maximum) can be used on a $350.00 maximum table.

Bet	*Target Area*	*Total Bet*	*Profit*
.20/.20/.20/.10	7–12,16–21,25–30,0–3	.70	.50/.50/.50/0
.30/.30/.20	7–12,25–30,0–3	1.50	.30/.30/–.10
.50/.50/.50	7–12,25–30,0–3	3.00	0/0/.50
1.00/1.00/.90	7–12,25–30,0–3	5.90	.10/.10/.40
1.90/1.90/1.70	7–12,25–30,0–3	11.40	0/0/.50

3.70/3.70/3.20	7–12,25–30,0–3	22.00	.20/.20/.40
6.00/6.00/2.00	7–12,25–30,0–00	36.00	0/0/0
11.50/11.50/9.80	7–12,25–30,0–00	68.80	.20/.20/.40
17.50/17.50	7–12,25–30	103.80	1.20/1.20
26.00/26.00	7–12,25–30	155.80	.20/.20
39.00/39.00	7–12,25–30	233.80	.20/.20
58.50/58.50	7–12,25–30	340.80	.20/.20

Okay, let's look at one more progression. Similiar to the previous progression, we will start with a large target area and reduce it as we go, except this time we will bet a fourth Double Row three times. As we know, these larger-base bets will accelerate our progression rapidly but give us more hits.

Let's look at the progression first:

Bet	*Target Area*	*Total Bet*	*Profit*
.25/.25/.25/.25	7–12,16–21,25–30,0–3	1.00	.50/.50/.50/.75
.50/.50/.50/.50	7–12,16–21,25–30,0–3	3.00	0/0/0/.50
1.50/1.50/1.50/1.25	7–12,16–21,25–30,0–3	8.75	.25/.25/.25/0
3.00/3.00/2.50	7–12,25–30,0–3	17.25	.75/.75/.25
5.50/5.50/4.75	7–12,25–30,0–3	33.00	0/0/.25
9.00/9.00/3.00	7–12,25–30,0–00	54.00	0/0/00
15.00/15.00/5.00	7–12,25–30,0–00	52.00	0/0/0
24.00/24.00/8.00	7–12,25–30,0–00	145.00	−1.00/−1.00/−1.00
40.50/40.50/13.50	7–12,25–30,0–00	239.50	3.50/3.50/3.50
60.00/60.00	7–12,25–30	359.50	.50/.50
90.00/90.00	7–12,25–30	539.50	.50/.50
135.00/135.00	7–12,25–30	809.50	.50/.50
200.00/200.00	7–12,25–30	1209.50	−9.50/−9.50

00	.75
29	1.25
1	2.00
21	2.50
11	3.00
10	3.50
13	
00	4.00
18	4.50
27	5.00
16	5.50
8	6.00
17	6.50
16	7.00
4	
20	7.00
25	7.50
5	
3	8.00
29	8.50
19	9.00
4	
30	9.00
18	9.50
0	10.25
33	
6	
11	10.50
33	
24	
4	
5	
27	10.50
6	
30	10.50
22	
24	
9	10.75
22	
7	10.75
14	
36	
7	11.00
11	11.50
27	12.00
19	12.50
18	13.00
28	13.50
16	14.00
28	14.50
2	15.25
7	15.75
31	
2	16.25
32	
27	16.25
3	17.00
8	17.50
8	18.00
24	
19	18.00
21	18.50
35	
7	18.50
25	19.00
33	
6	
31	
12	19.75
5	
1	20.25
32	
25	20.25
1	21.00
35	
25	21.00
34	
28	21.00
5	
23	
12	21.25
23	
7	21.25
1	22.00
8	22.50
1	23.25
31	
23	
31	
30	24.00
7	24.50
00	25.25
33	
3	25.75
3	26.50
21	27.00

6
6
3 27.50
9 28.00
14
28 28.00
17 28.50
23
35
26 28.75
33
8 28.75
27 29.25
31
16 29.25
8 29.75
31
22
27 30.00
8 30.50
19 31.00
11 31.50
3 32.25
29 32.75
24
24
22
21

TOTAL 77/123

7 .50
32
24
9 .75
5
19 .75
1 1.50
0 2.25
22
26 2.25
6
7 2.25
33
18 2.25
16 2.75
11 3.25
24
30 3.25
26 3.75
13
27 3.75
13
17 3.75
8 4.25
8 4.75
7 5.25
6
21 5.25
5
10 5.25
8 5.75
1 6.50

19 7.00
7 7.50
18 8.00
4

TOTAL 24/36

15	
24	
17	.25
26	.75
25	1.25
25	1.75
13	
8	1.75
18	2.25
7	2.75
30	3.25
1	4.00
9	4.50
11	5.00
8	5.50
5	
35	
7	5.75
7	6.25
4	
5	
6	
30	7.00
27	7.50
32	
7	7.50
4	
3	8.00
25	8.50
7	9.00
12	9.50
4	
20	9.50
7	10.00
16	10.50
5	
6	
00	10.50
25	11.00

TOTAL 26/39

0	.75
0	1.50
0	2.25
15	
21	2.25
8	2.75
19	3.25
14	
14	
29	3.50
15	
12	3.50
24	
14	
00	3.50
18	4.00
4	
7	4.00
6	
15	
35	
36	
1	4.75
9	5.25
7	5.75
12	6.25
18	6.75
19	7.25
13	
25	7.25
31	
29	7.25
24	
16	7.25
20	7.75
28	8.25
28	8.75
9	9.25
3	10.00
1	10.75
30	11.25
5	

TOTAL 27/42

36	
4	
0	0
30	.50
36	
17	.50
12	1.00
26	1.50
26	2.00
23	
20	2.00
33	
20	2.00
19	2.50
11	3.00
00	3.75
16	4.25
8	4.75
20	5.25
0	6.00
00	6.75
32	
4	
35	
27	7.50
2	8.25
14	
0	8.75
0	9.50
2	10.25
22	
5	
23	
26	11.00
10	11.50
00	12.25
00	13.00
15	
18	13.00
15	
27	13.00
15	
27	13.00
31	
3	13.50
29	14.00

TOTAL 30/46

22	
13	
30	.25
12	.75
32	
4	
10	1.00
34	
3	1.50
19	2.00
00	2.75
7	3.25
10	3.75
32	
18	3.75
11	4.25
30	4.75
28	5.25
32	
11	5.25
12	5.75
12	6.25
30	6.75
4	
22	
24	
1	7.00
2	7.75
14	
00	8.25
1	9.00
5	
27	9.00
9	9.50
14	
22	
2	9.50
7	10.00

TOTAL 24/38

12	.50
7	1.00
33	
36	
3	1.00
20	1.50
15	
23	
21	1.75
7	2.25
15	
5	
19	2.50
00	3.25
25	3.75
14	
36	
4	
16	
3	4.00
5	
30	4.00
6	
14	
24	
19	
14	
30	4.00
1	4.75
4	

TOTAL 13/30

33	
22	
31	
11	.75
0	1.50
14	
11	1.50
36	
1	2.00
21	2.50
13	
25	2.50
2	3.25
30	3.75
25	4.25
7	4.75

TOTAL 10/16

7	.50
2	1.25
29	1.75
9	2.25
25	2.75
32	
29	2.75
2	3.50
30	4.00
21	4.50
9	5.00
9	5.50
8	6.00
16	6.50
2	7.25
9	7.75
20	8.25
18	8.75
18	9.25
0	10.00
5	
36	
30	10.25
35	
12	10.25
28	10.75
27	11.25
TOTAL	23/27

4	
36	
3	0
19	.50
20	1.00
10	1.50
27	2.00
9	2.50
17	3.00
35	
32	
2	3.00
12	3.50
34	
1	4.00
9	4.50
TOTAL	11/16

Number	Amount
2	.75
9	1.25
24	
2	1.75
33	
9	1.75
3	2.50
28	3.00
16	3.50
10	4.00
5	
19	4.00
36	
35	
25	4.25
23	
20	4.25
3	5.00
0	5.75
0	6.50
0	7.25
6	
14	
1	7.25
4	
30	7.25
20	7.75
7	8.25
28	8.75
27	9.25
00	10.00
3	10.75

Number	Amount
3	11.50
15	
11	11.50
0	12.25
8	12.75
3	13.50
10	14.00
32	
14	
15	
24	
15	
10	14.00

TOTAL 30/45

30	.50
31	
10	.50
27	1.00
19	1.50
17	2.00
10	2.50
0	3.25
2	4.00
17	4.50
35	
16	4.50
12	5.00
25	5.50
1	6.25
15	
0	6.75
16	7.25
0	8.00
5	
31	
0	8.00
15	
12	8.00
00	8.75
00	9.50
21	10.00
3	10.75
1	11.50
4	
36	
17	11.75
9	12.25
15	
28	12.25
30	12.75
5	
34	

TOTAL 27/38

8	.50
34	
26	.50
33	
17	.50
2	1.25
31	
18	1.25
12	1.75
30	2.25
8	2.75
17	3.25
12	3.75
5	
34	
19	4.00
4	
3	4.50
12	5.00
32	
7	5.00
8	5.50
26	6.00
31	
32	
15	
10	6.75
31	
6	
4	
7	7.50
23	

35	
24	
30	8.25
6	
8	8.25
32	
17	8.25
3	9.00
33	
00	9.50
16	10.00
9	10.50
10	11.00
34	
18	11.00
31	
35	
7	11.25
28	11.75
TOTAL	29/51

9	.50
12	1.00
35	
31	
12	1.25
6	
28	1.25
1	2.00
0	2.75
3	3.50
00	4.25
33	
16	4.25
32	
8	4.25
TOTAL	10/15

16	.50
4	
28	.50
27	1.00
22	
18	1.00
10	1.50
21	2.00
2	2.75
25	
3	3.25
11	3.75
14	
3	4.25
7	4.75
2	5.50
26	6.00
27	6.50
27	7.00
21	7.50
00	8.25
5	
20	8.25
15	
27	8.25
30	8.75
12	9.25
30	9.75
29	10.25
32	
11	10.25

TOTAL 24/31

10	.50
16	1.00
1	1.75
20	2.25
11	2.75
5	
23	
24	
27	3.50
9	4.00
33	
17	4.00
13	
18	4.00
9	4.50
14	

TOTAL 10/16

8	.50
1	1.25
19	1.75
0	2.50
23	
25	2.50
17	3.00
17	3.50
4	
33	
21	3.75
36	
12	3.75
19	4.25
8	4.75
7	5.25
27	5.75
19	6.25
22	
11	6.25
12	6.75
8	7.25
16	7.75
1	8.50
0	9.25
19	9.75

TOTAL 21/26

29	.50
35	
9	.50
20	1.00
6	
10	1.00
34	
18	1.00
8	1.50
12	2.00
31	
26	2.00
4	
12	2.00
13	
26	2.00
27	2.50
36	
0	3.00
20	3.50
00	4.25
12	4.75
19	5.25
24	
5	
18	5.50
11	6.00
21	6.50
26	7.00
10	7.50
29	8.00
3	8.75

00	9.50
20	10.00
7	10.50
35	
11	10.50
10	11.00
11	11.50
16	12.00
0	12.75
24	
2	13.25
9	13.75
3	14.50
32	
7	14.50
13	
21	14.50
23	
31	
12	14.75
10	15.25
27	15.75

TOTAL 39/54

<u>9</u>	.50
5	
<u>19</u>	.50
<u>1</u>	1.25
<u>0</u>	2.00
22	
<u>26</u>	2.00
6	
<u>7</u>	2.00
33	
<u>18</u>	2.00
<u>16</u>	2.50
<u>11</u>	3.00
24	
<u>30</u>	3.00
<u>26</u>	3.50
13	
<u>27</u>	3.50
13	
<u>17</u>	3.50
<u>8</u>	4.00
<u>8</u>	4.50
<u>7</u>	5.00
6	
<u>21</u>	5.00
5	
<u>10</u>	5.00
<u>8</u>	5.50
<u>1</u>	6.25
<u>19</u>	6.75
<u>7</u>	7.25
<u>18</u>	7.75
4	

TOTAL 23/33

<u>10</u>	.50
13	
13	
35	
<u>3</u>	.75
24	
<u>18</u>	.75
4	
36	
<u>2</u>	.75
<u>25</u>	1.25
13	
<u>26</u>	1.25
<u>18</u>	1.75
31	
<u>12</u>	1.75

TOTAL 8/16

Not bad: 486 out of 739—a little less than 66 percent. And, as before, the longest losing streak is five—twice. But, regrettably, we don't win as much money—only $204.75. Then why would we want to bet this progression? Remember, all the spin sequences in this book actually occured. But none of them will ever repeat exactly the same way again. You will never know what the next spin sequence will be; you can never know. All the various progressions in this book are designed to give you a choice based on what you see happening on the wheel and what your starting bankroll is. If you have a smaller bankroll, you might like the idea of more hits with less money than would the person who has a big enough bankroll to survive slightly longer losing streaks.

My opinion, and I've said this before, is that you should expand your betting with casino money. I would play the following progression:

If possible, start with the dime table progression on page 000. Play no more than two hours at a stretch. As much as I hate to admit this, you can get bored playing the progressions in this book—even though you are winning. If you're bored, you'll make mistakes—very costly mistakes if you miss a number during one of the progressions. Using this dime table progression, you should win approximately 20 to 24 cents per spin; on a table that's not too busy, you should average about a spin a minute. Let's calculate the total winnings for the two hours: 120 spins X $.20 per spin = $24.00. (Bear in mind that these are just approximations; each spin sequence is different.) When you are comfortably ahead, take your original bankroll and *put it back in the bank*. Take your profits and move up to the quarter table.

7

Summation

The thing I like about this system is, obviously, the fact that it wins! In fact, all the variations win—to varying degrees of success with different base amounts risked. As I stated before, I originally started out betting the 3-3-1 variation, but one big loser made me revise my thinking.

I'm not a wealthy man. During the particularly galling experience of losing nine 3-3-1 spins in a row at the Palace Station Casino in Las Vegas (the time I got so angry that I threw the paper away, so the sequence is not listed here), I noticed that the 2 and 3 had both come up during that run of bad luck. It was then that I reexamined the wheel and noticed that there they were—the 1 and the 2—right there, adjacent to the two groups that I was betting! Then I noticed that the 3—which had also hit one time during that bad run—naturally fit the betting pattern, although it's not really in the grouping. Armed with this information, I looked at the spin sequences I'd bet up until my big losing session and, sure enough, the 1, 2, and 3 hit often enough to lower (at least up until then) the consecutive loss totals down to no more than six in a row—a trend which lowers the initial money I have to risk.

After I began playing the Three Double-Row variation, much to my happiness, I noticed that not only were the losing streaks per session lessened, but there no longer was such a thing as even one big losing session. As you saw, only twice did the spin sequences I'd earlier played using the 3-3-1 lose—and both times for only four units. I was onto something. When I went and played the 1–3 spin session—and won—I knew I had a winning system.

But I wanted more. I looked at the spin sequences and noticed how often the 16 through 21 hit. That's when I experimented (successfully) with the Four Double-Row variations.

I've never bet the Two Double-Row or One Double-Row variations. I've simply included them for your information. It's been interesting to me that they both win. But it's also been dissatisfying to note that in each of the variations (other than the basic Three Double-Row), there is also at least one big losing session. I don't like that at any time, but can live with it for a risk *if I'm using casino money*. Therefore, I recommend you start with one of the Three Double-Row combination variations.

No matter what variation you use, our spin sequences indicate that you'll probably lose two times out of twenty, but the Three Double-Row or the combinations will minimize those losses, too.

Once you've won enough money—enough to give you two sessions of 3-3-1 bets (in the case of my recommended betting progression, that would be $234.00)—try one 3-3-1 session. If it hits, it's a bigger winner than the Three Double-Row. But, don't forget, if it misses (as it will 10 percent of the time), you'll suffer a bigger loss. You'll never know when you'll have those two losing sessions. With bad luck it could be the first two times you change variations. If it is, just go back to the Three Double-Row or a combination and earn enough to try it again... or stick with the Three Double-Row or the combination and earn, earn, earn. When you've earned enough, increase the money amount of the progression.

Also, bear table limits in mind. If you want to start with a $.50 unit, you can't play at a $.50 minimum table, because the minimum inside is $2.00, and $.50 times three Double-Rows is only $1.50; you must bet this level at a $.25 minimum table where the inside minimum is $1.00. You can't bet this betting progression with a $.25 unit unless you find one of the rare $.10 minimum tables in play today.

8

Final Thoughts

Since I've both created this system and played around with it much more than you, I'll pass along some final recommendations and two final requests. What you do with this information is up to you.

RECOMMENDATIONS

Unlike systems for other casino games, where you need to be playing the game to try out the system and if you are in the game everything is different; whether you are playing or not, the roulette spin sequence should remain relatively the same. Go to a casino and see whether all I've written is true. But remember, don't just look at a number board. Number boards aren't always accurate. In roulette, seeing is believing!

Find a friendly table. Find a table where our numbers seem to hit consistently over a period of time. All roulette wheels are balanced differently; find one balanced in your favor.

Start conservatively. It could be just your luck that in your first or second session you hit a bad run. Besides, it's always a good idea to increase your betting scheme only when you are ahead and playing with the casino's money. *This applies to every casino game.*

Limit your winnings per session, too. Have a cutoff point. Most books on other gambling systems recommend you take a break when you've doubled your money. Sounds as good as any other idea to me. On the other hand, it's best to press when you're winning, not when you're losing. If you start out a winner (which you should do 90 percent of the time), when the luck seems to be turning, get out with some profit!

It makes no difference if you make the 5-to-1 Double-Row bet or put one check on each of the six numbers, nor does it matter if you make the Double-Row bet or two Single-Row bets on the same numbers (I've looked at both these possibilities). If you bet 6 checks on the Double-Row, you win 30 checks; if you bet 1 check on each of the same six numbers, the winning number pays 35 checks but you lose the other 5 checks—35 minus 5 equals the same 30 checks.

Conglomerate. Don't have a big enough bankroll to get started? Call your friends, explain the system, and pool your money.

Create your own betting progressions based on your bankroll and the table you'll be playing on. But be forewarned! You can get hooked on it. That's the voice of experience talking to you.

REQUESTS

First, don't share this information with your friends (unless you need their money to increase your bankroll). You spent the money for the book, you make the profit. Why do I request this?

Contrary to what you may think, it is not greed based upon book sales; it's greed based upon the fact that I bet this system myself. If too many people are playing this system and winning too much money, it won't be long before the casinos realize that their only option is to change the wheel and eliminate the sequential numbering groups that are the basis for this system. If that happens, both you and I are out.

Second, Dealers work for "tokes" (gaming terminology for tips). If you win, and you will, don't forget the dealers. A tip of 5 percent to 10 percent is nice. (Good tokes will lessen the dealer's stress when the floorperson begins asking them why, all of a sudden, the roulette wheel is taking such big losses.)

And finally:

GOOD LUCK!